Coloring Yourself Calm, Volume 3

ADULT COLORING BOOK

By

JEFFREY LITTORNO

Copyright © 2015

.

INTRODUCTION

Here we are on the opening page of another book in the *Coloring Yourself Calm* series of adult coloring books. Thanks for coming back!

I'm sure that you didn't buy this book to read my ramblings on the benefits of coloring. Don't worry, I'll keep it short.

Coloring is relaxing and therapeutic. Just try to be in a bad mood when you're coloring! The very act of coloring seems to melt away the stress.

Each mandala in this book was designed to keep the *colorer* occupied for an hour or two. Of course, there is no time limit. The only important thing is to have fun.

Once again, thanks for coming back and hope to see you for the next book!

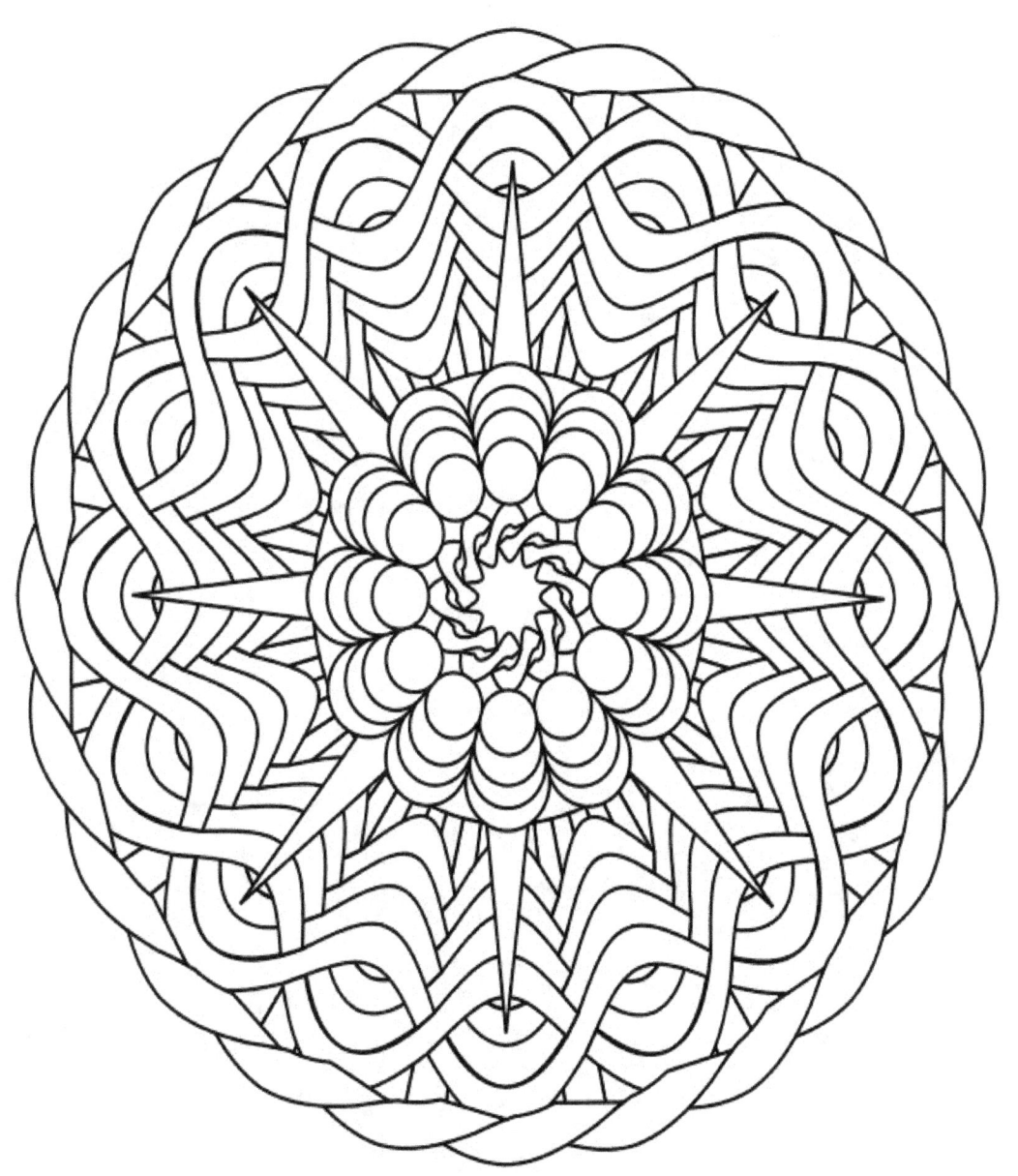

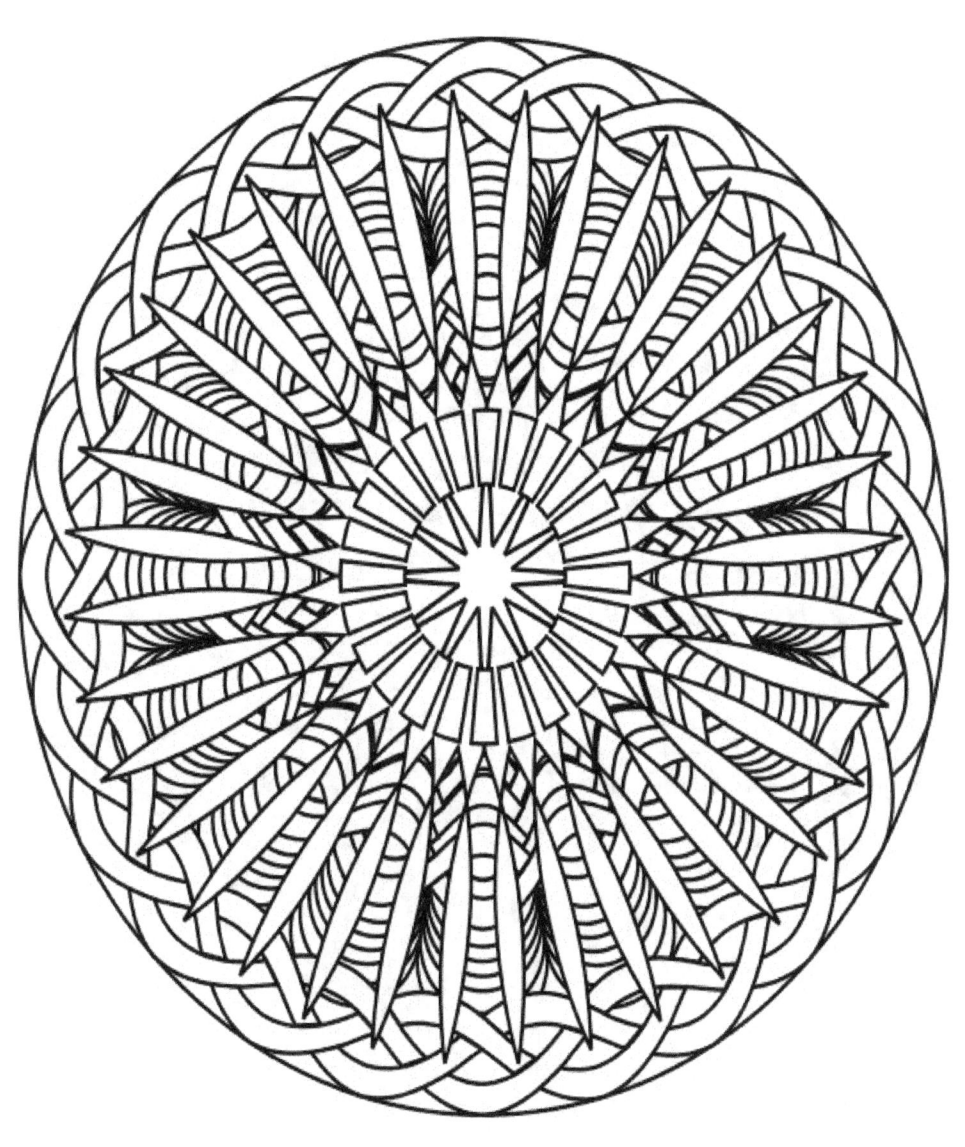

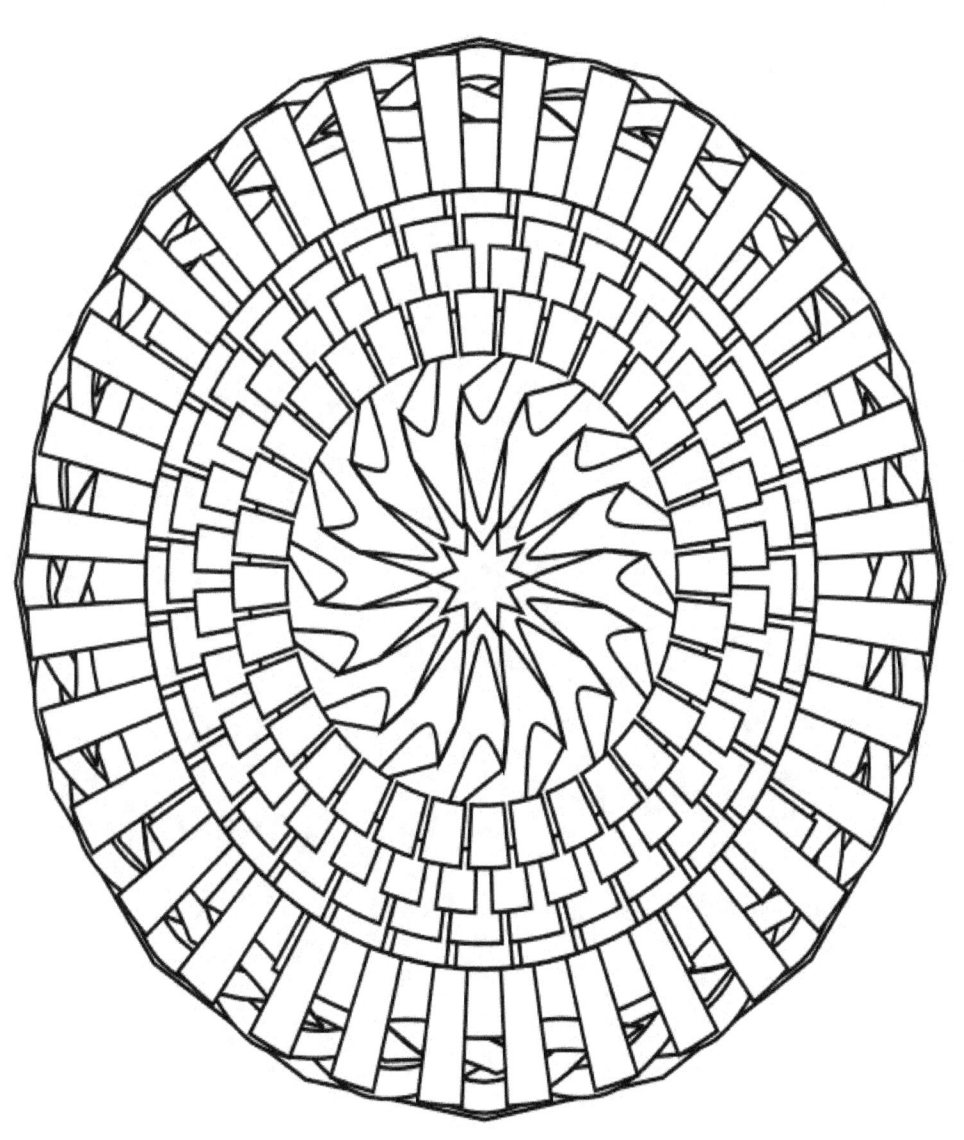

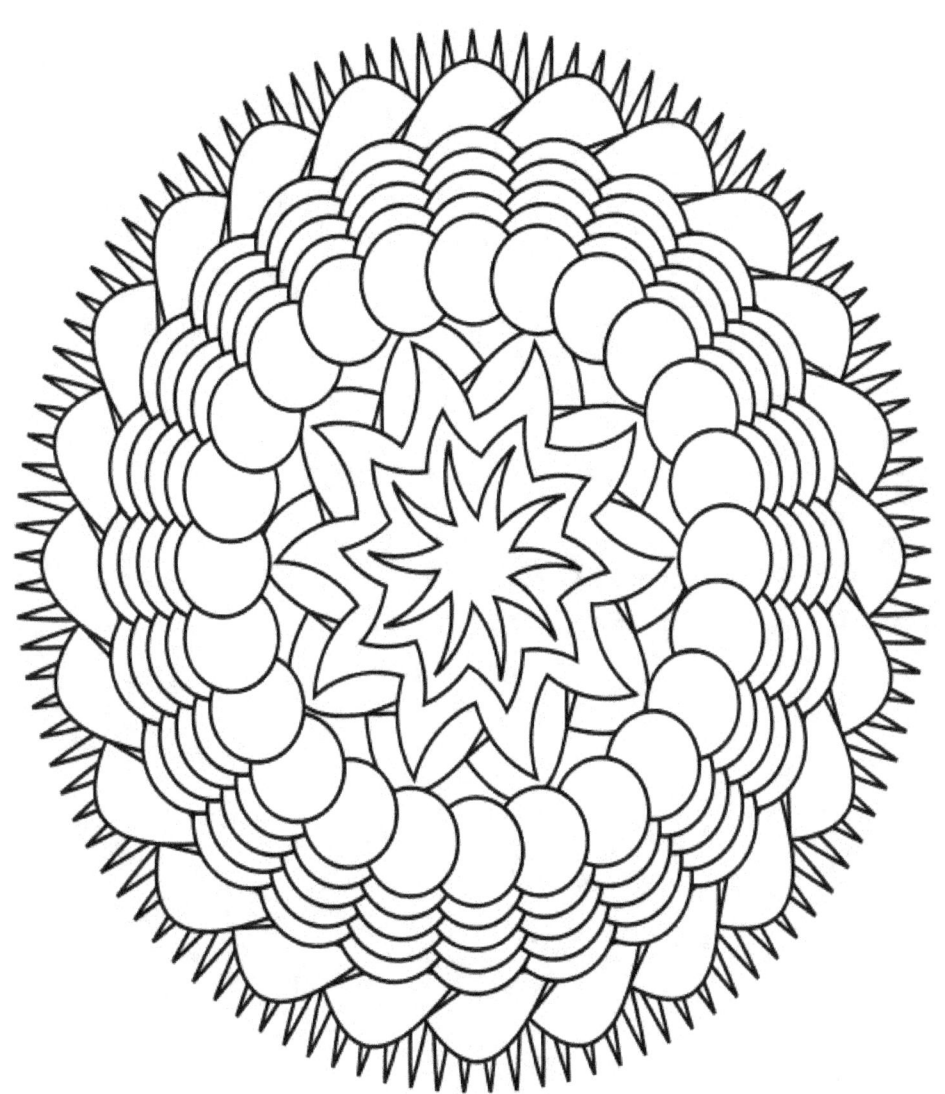

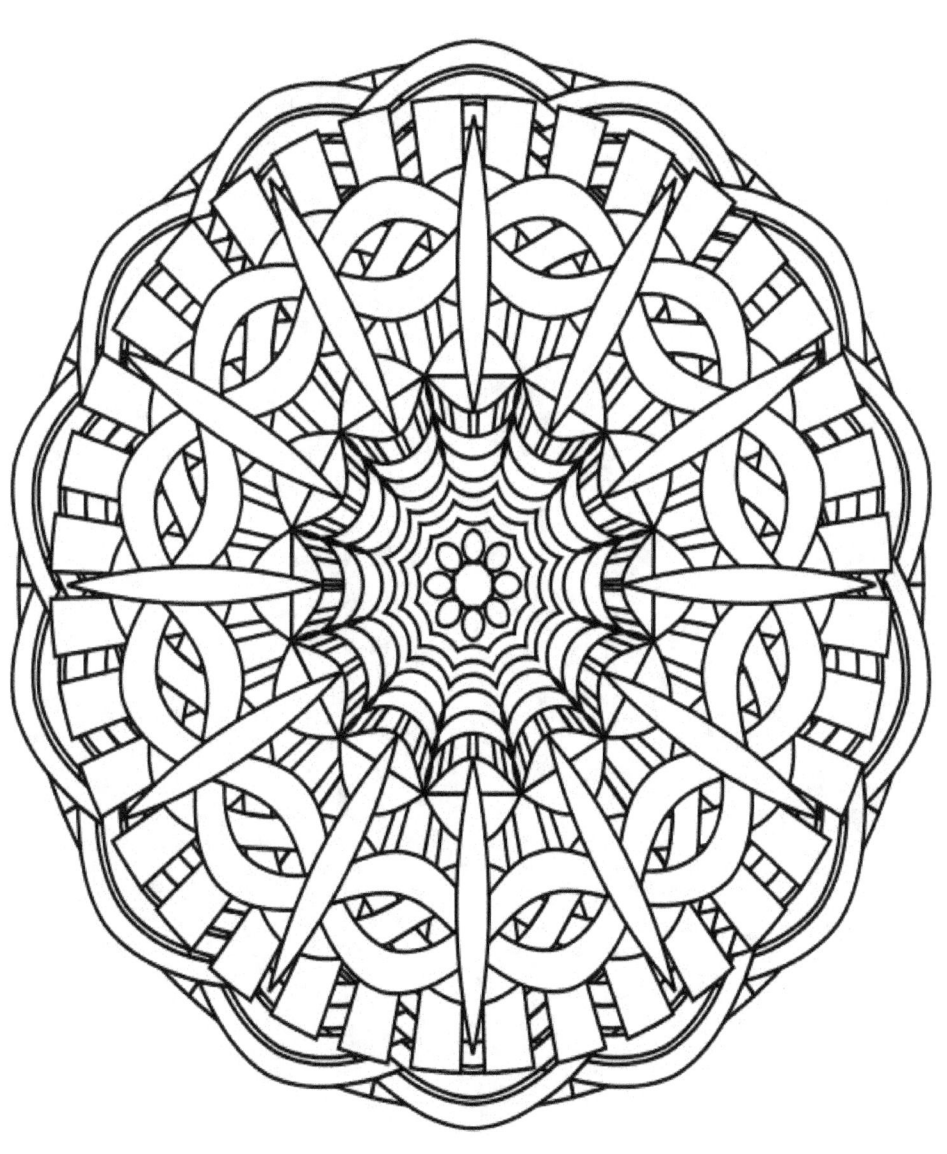

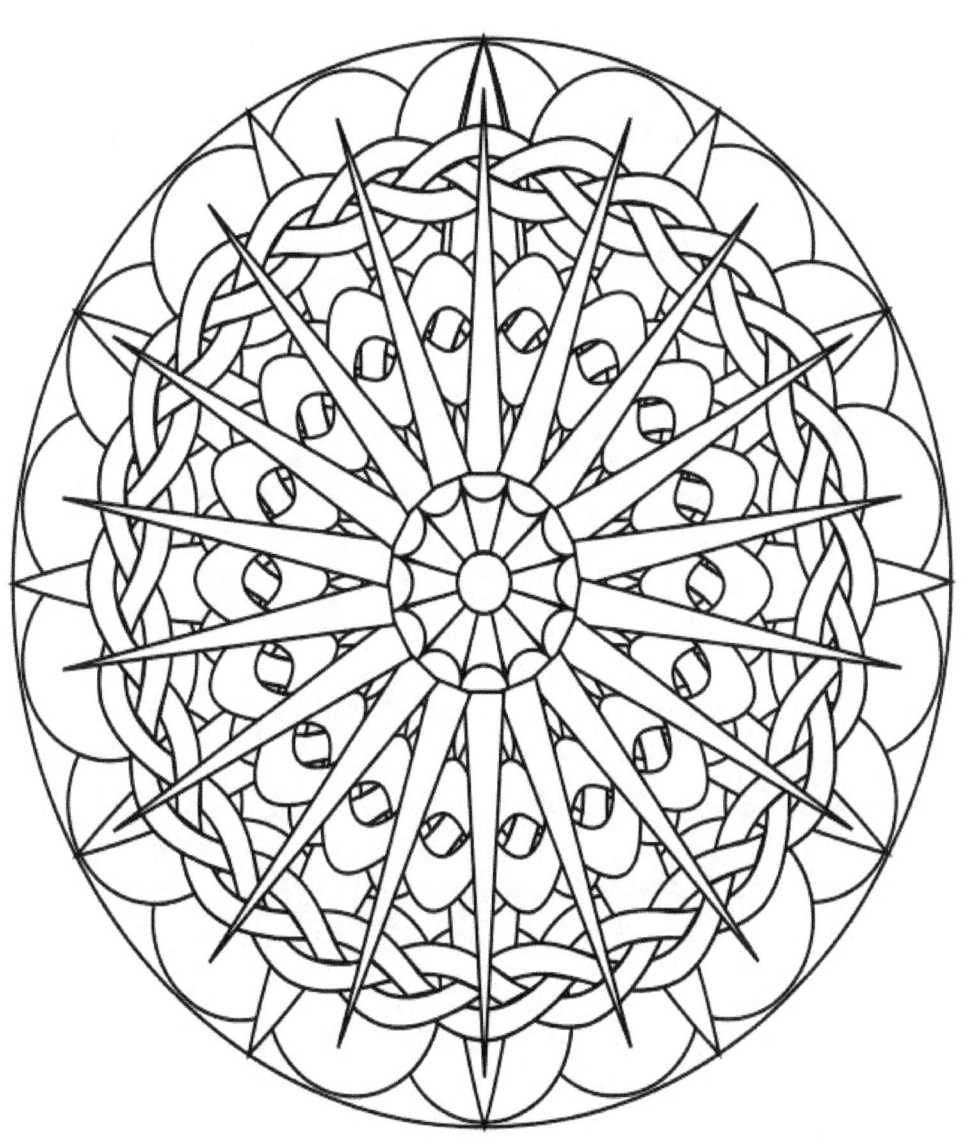

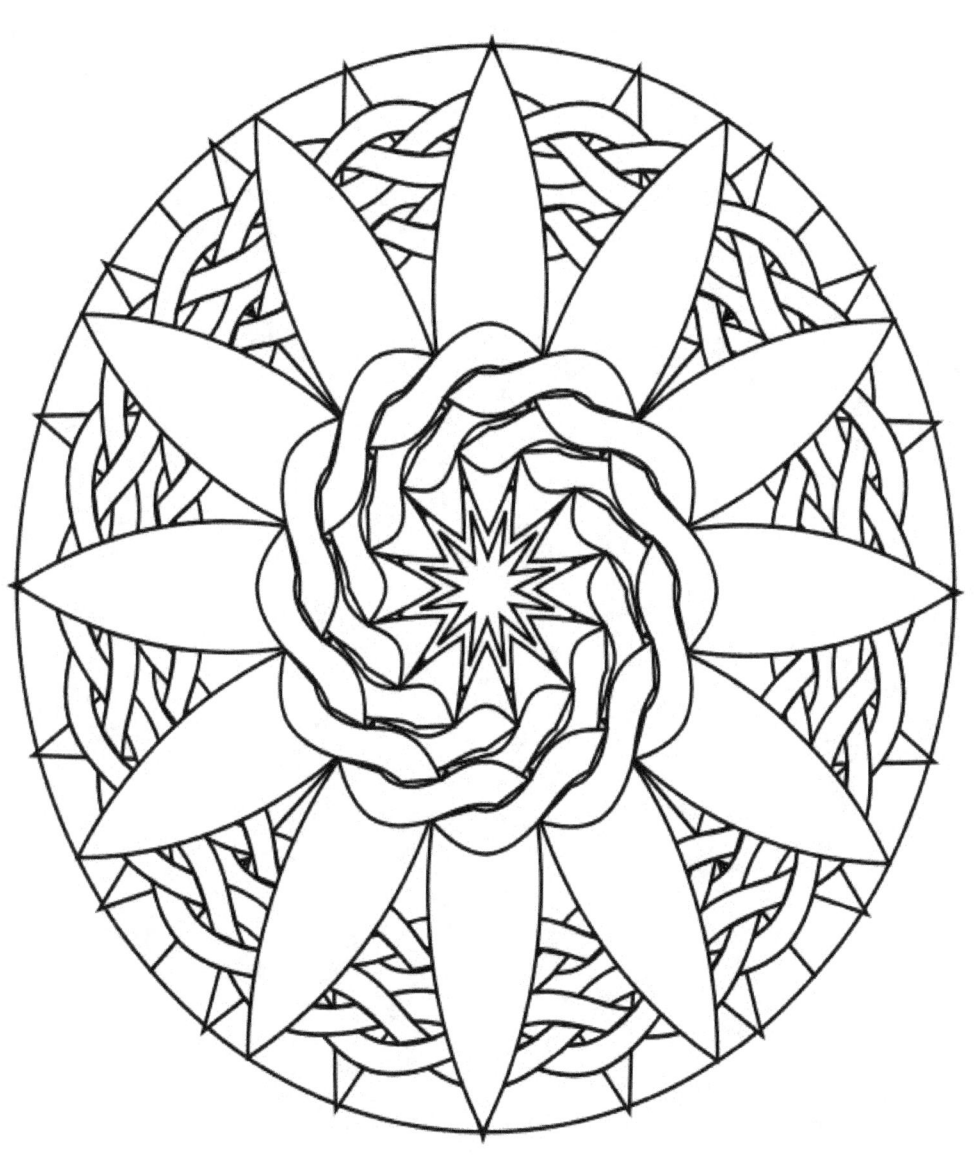

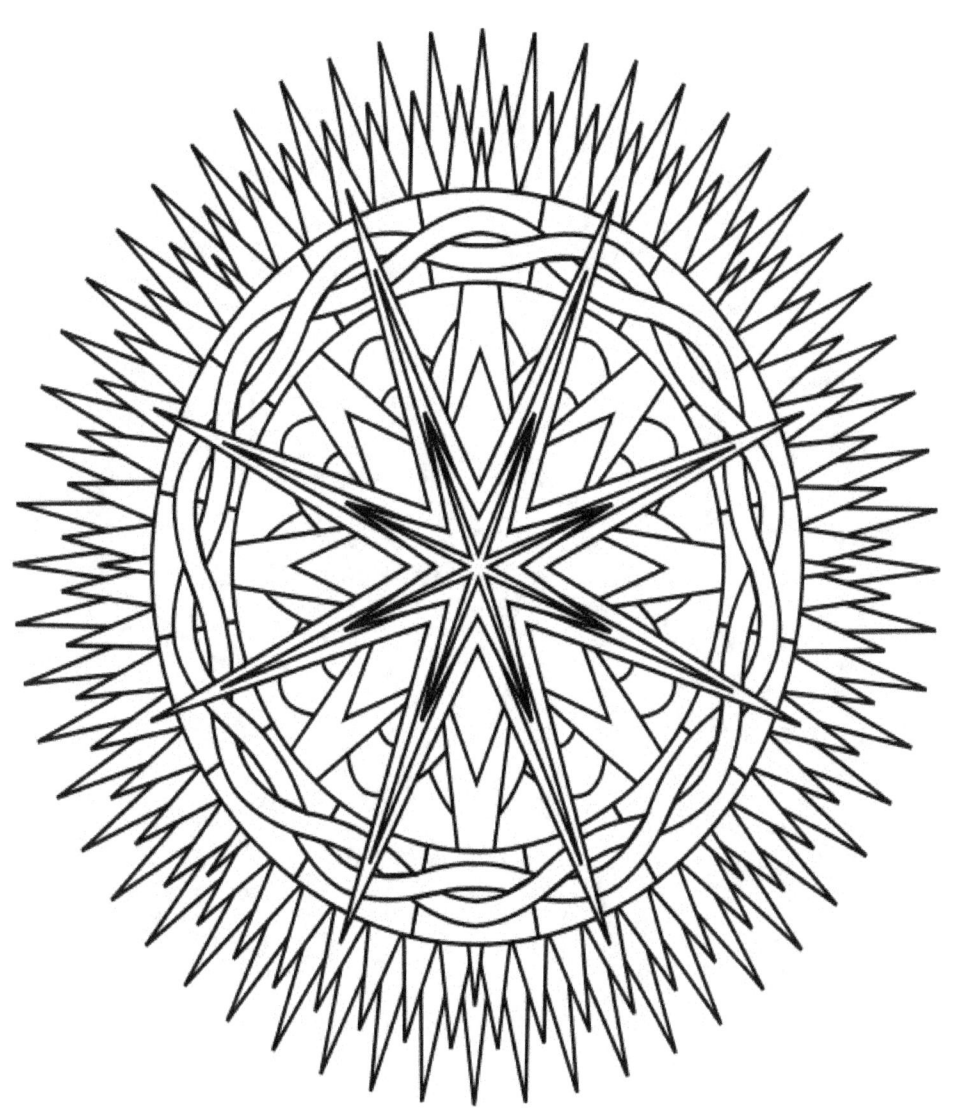

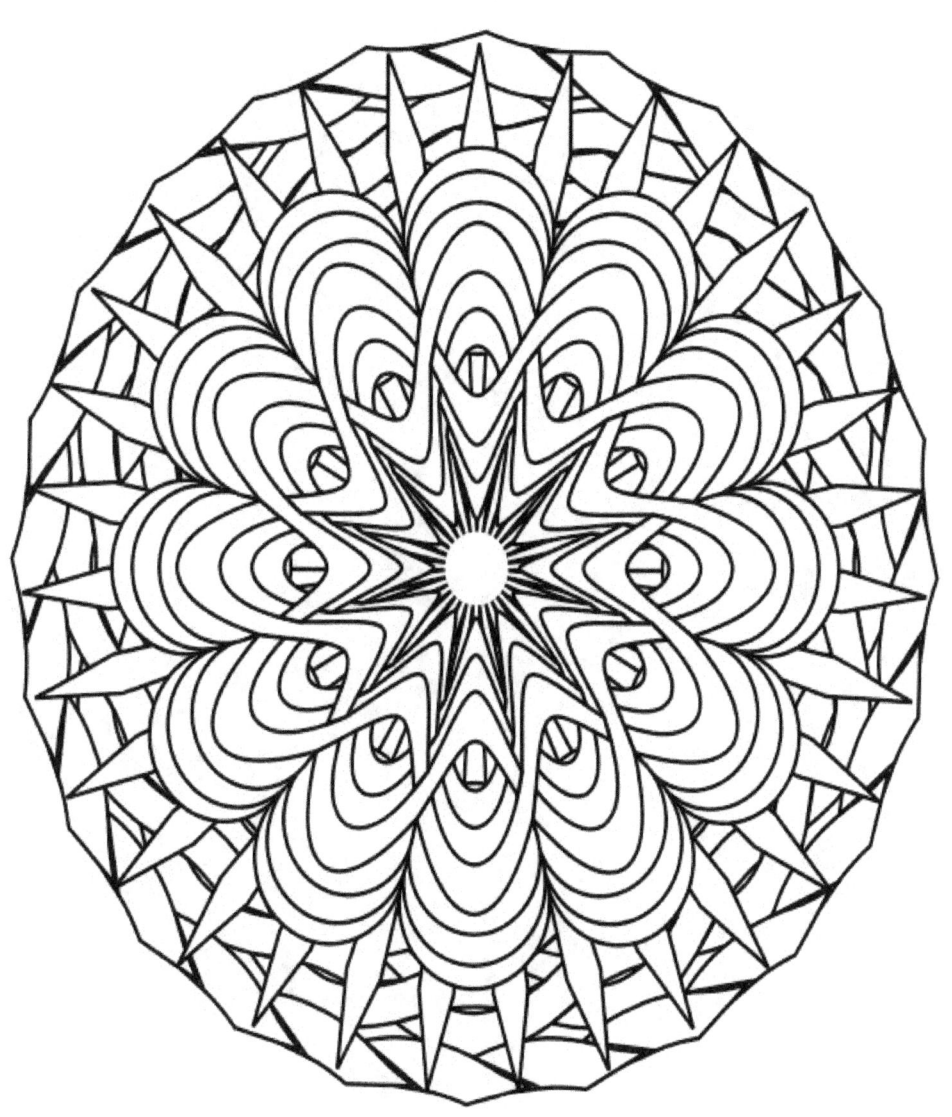

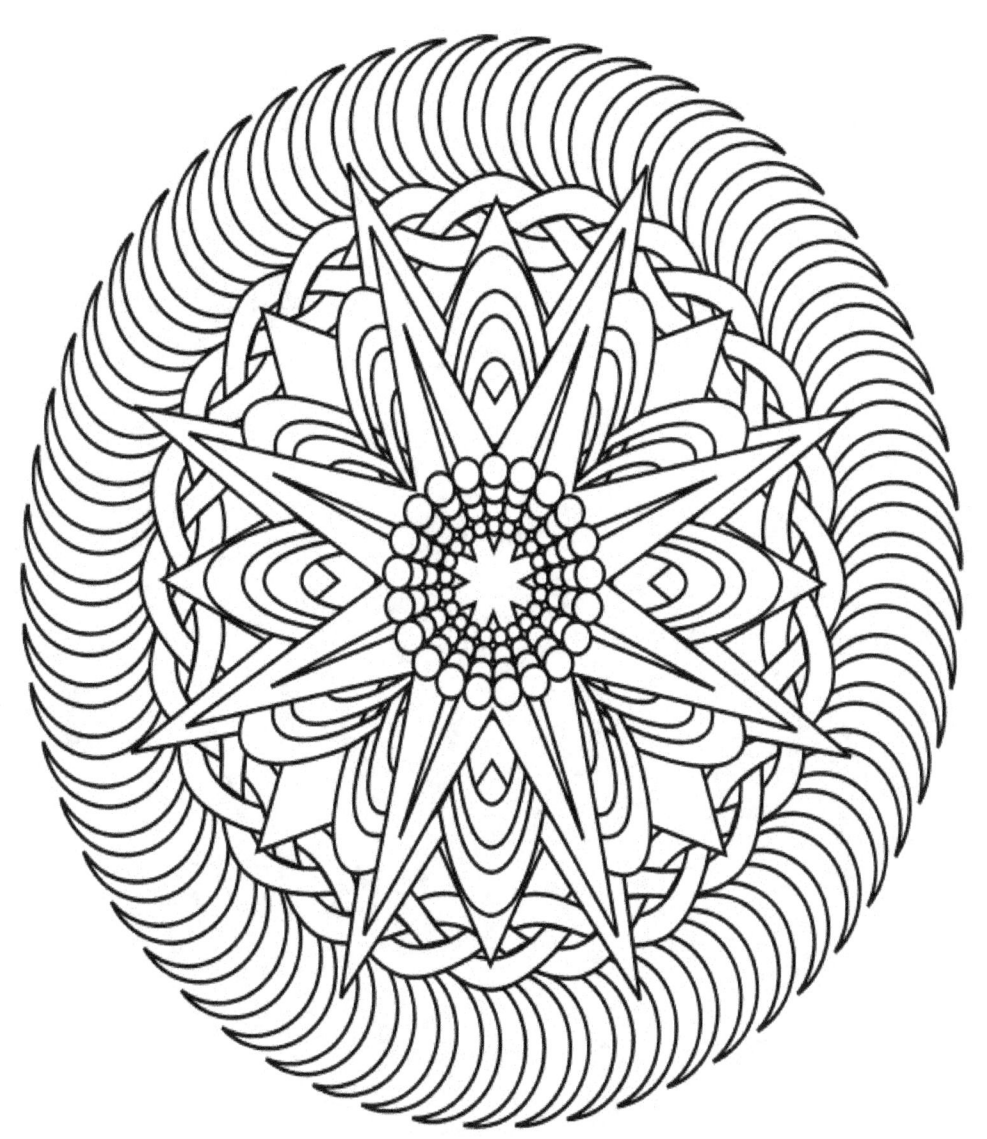

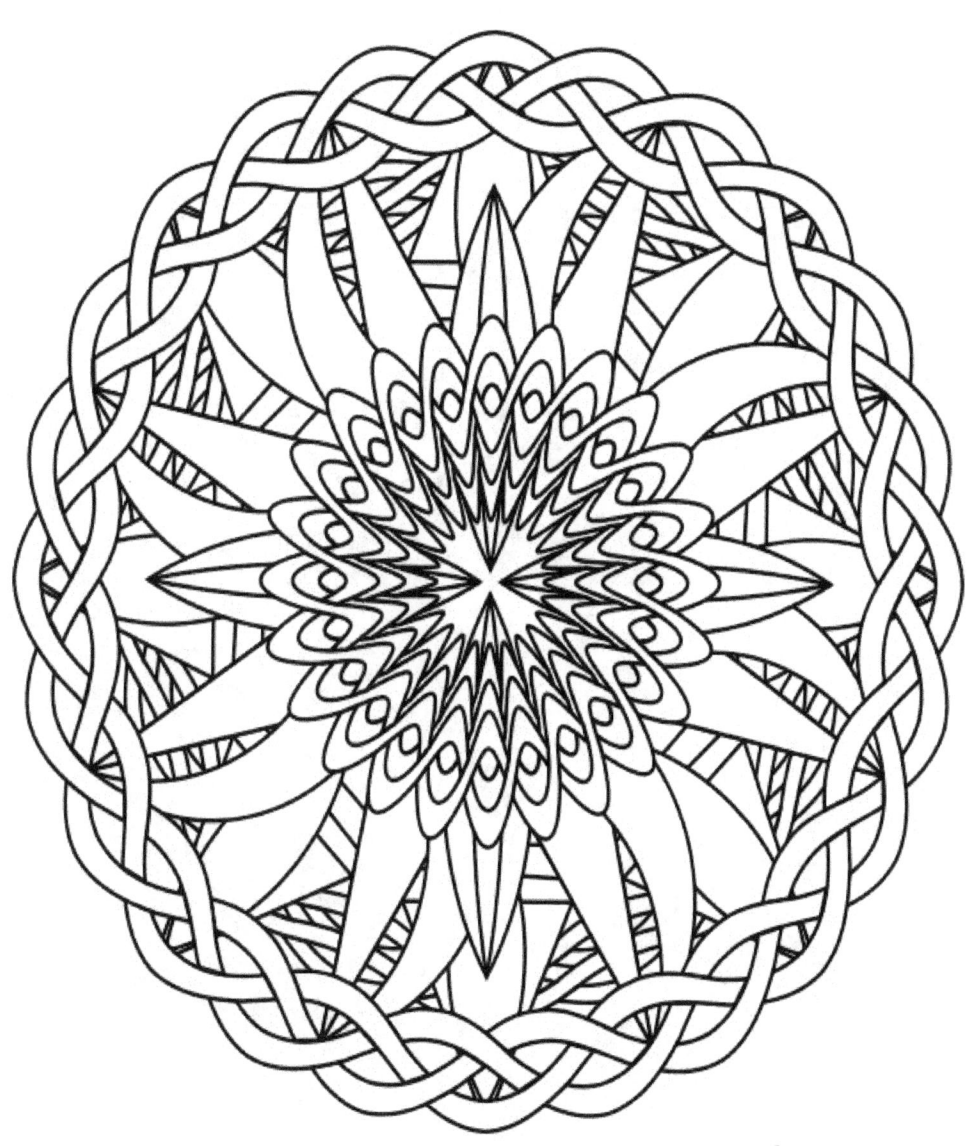

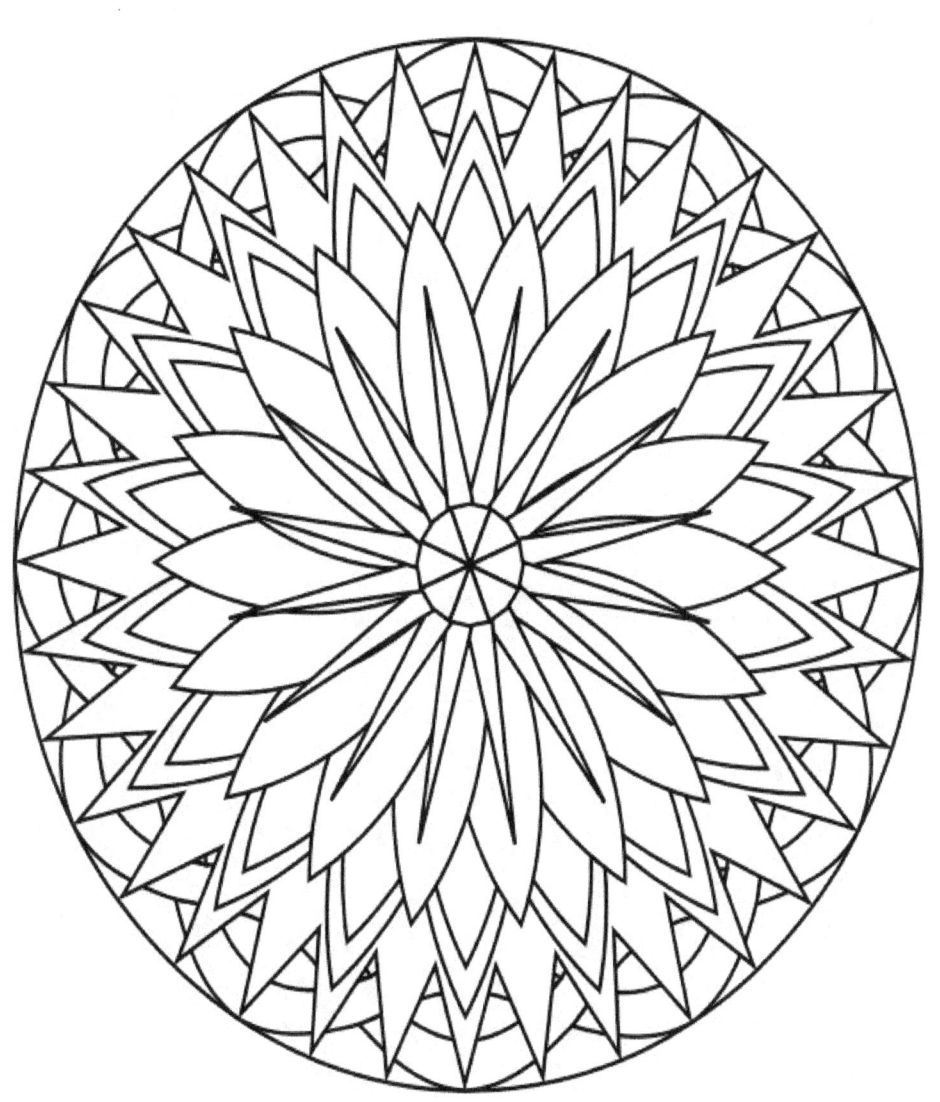

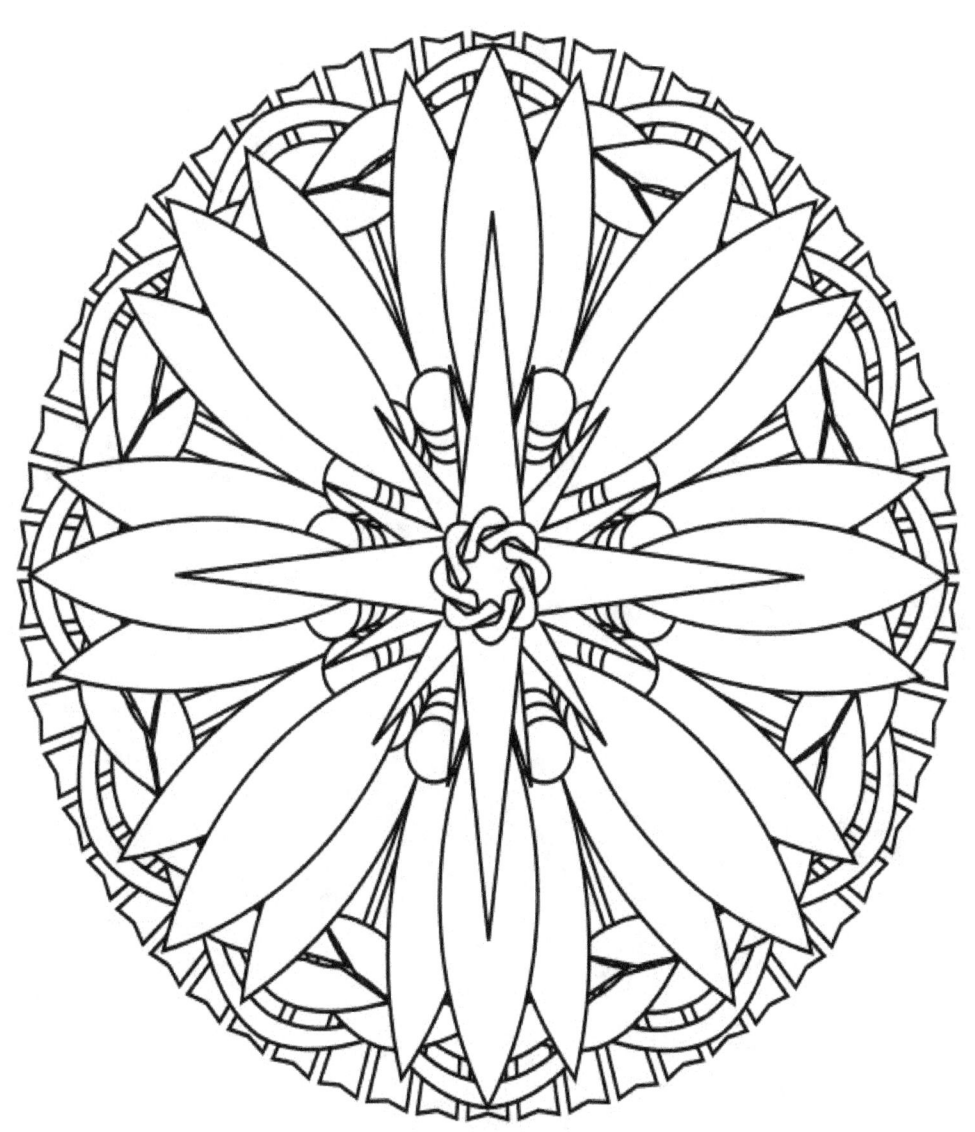

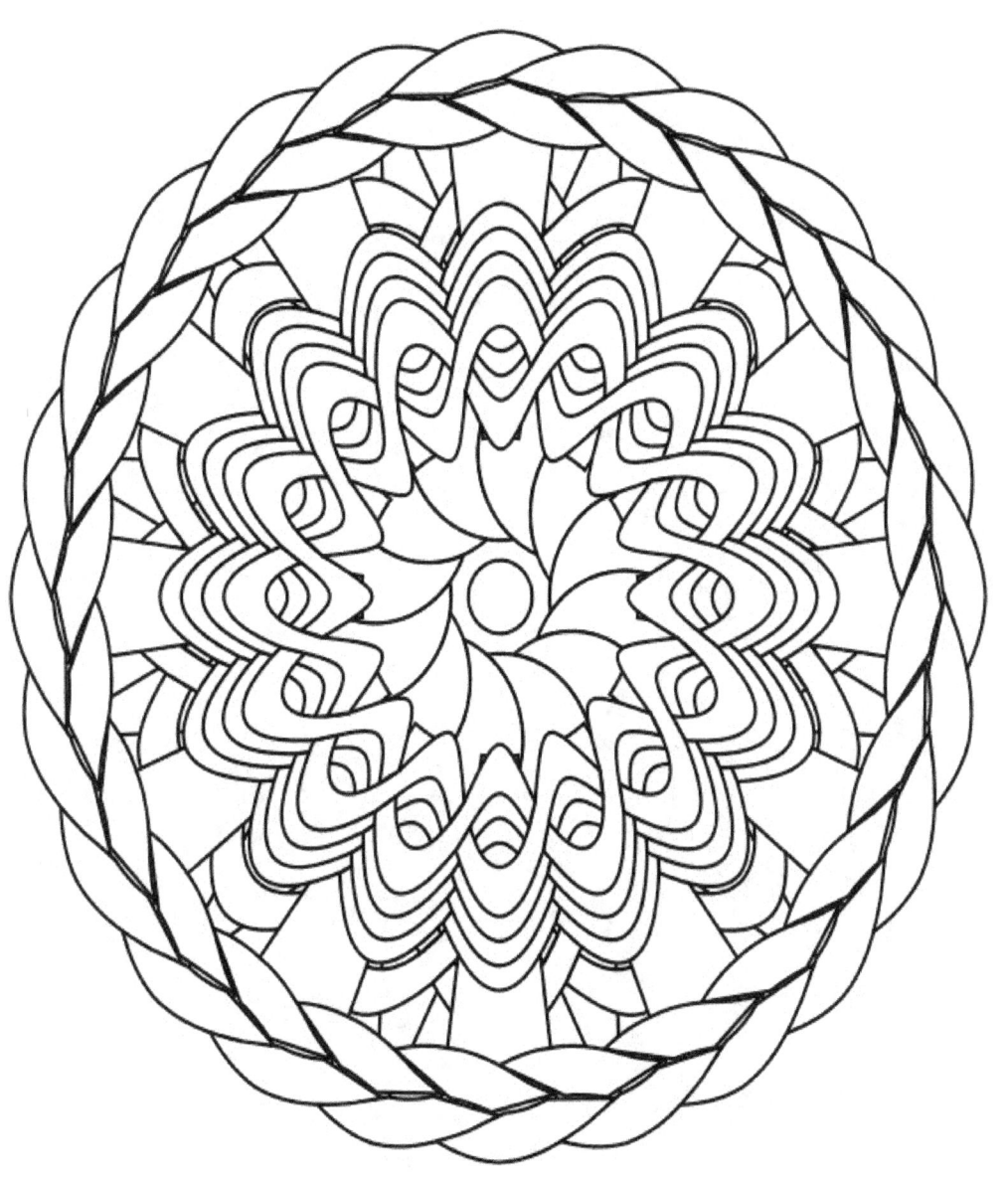

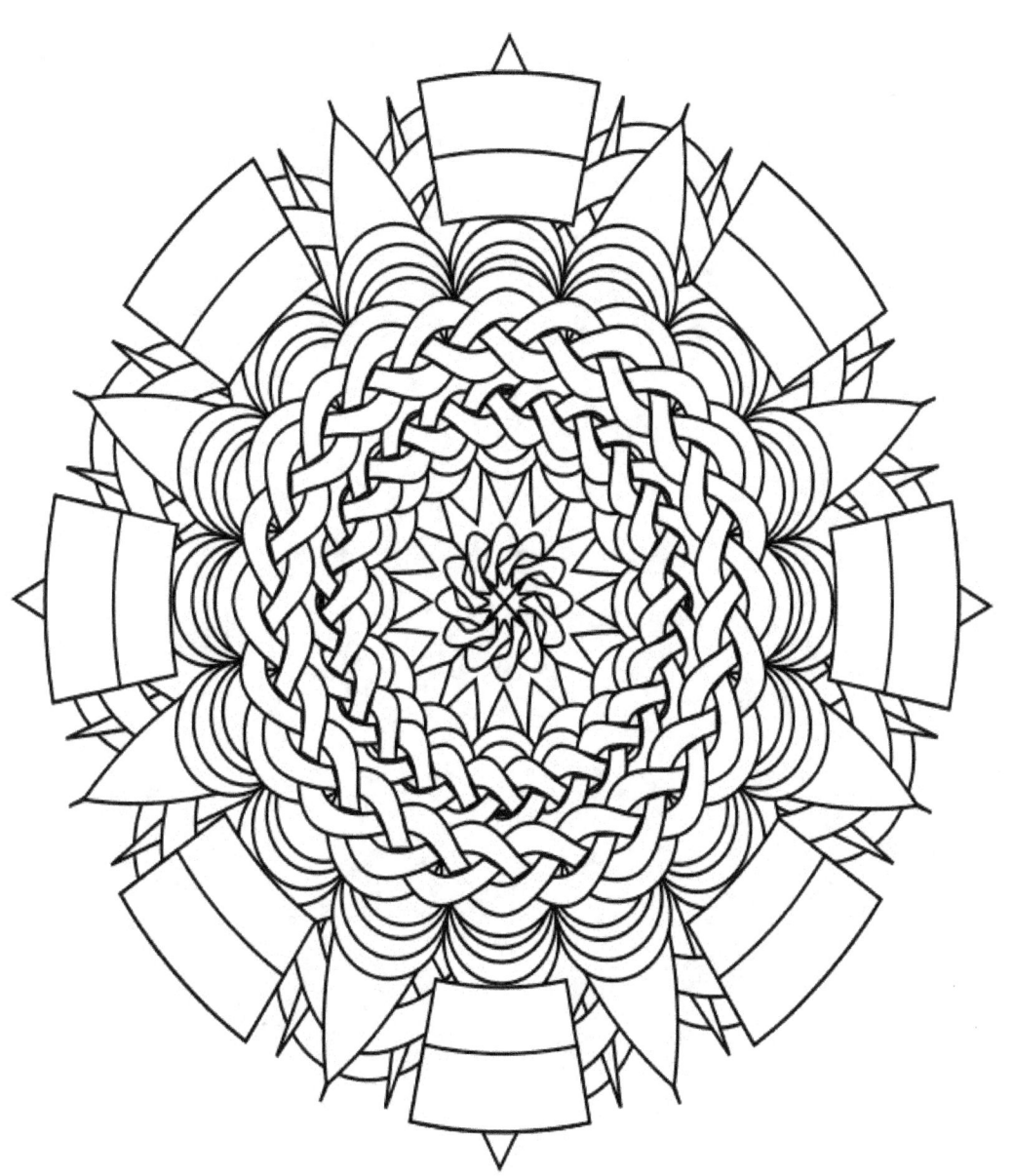

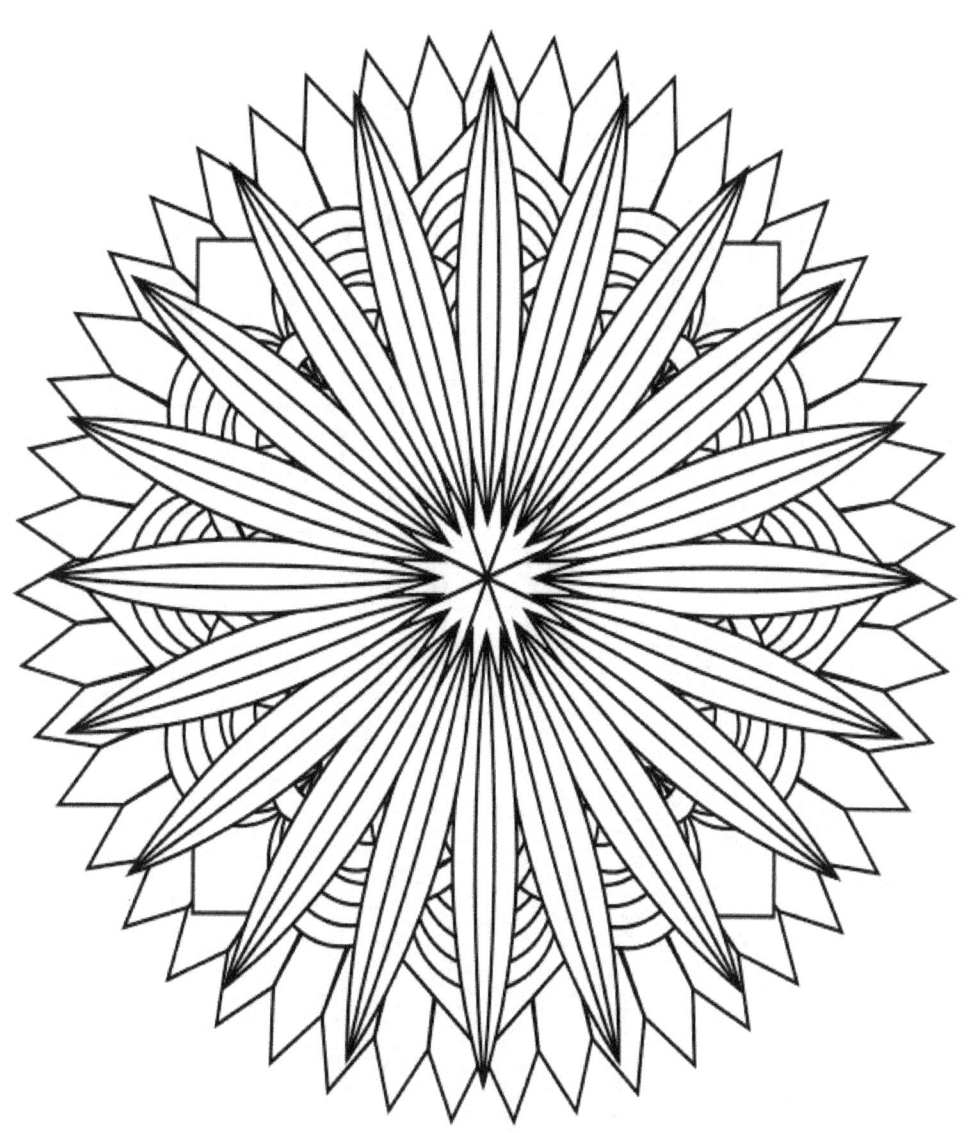

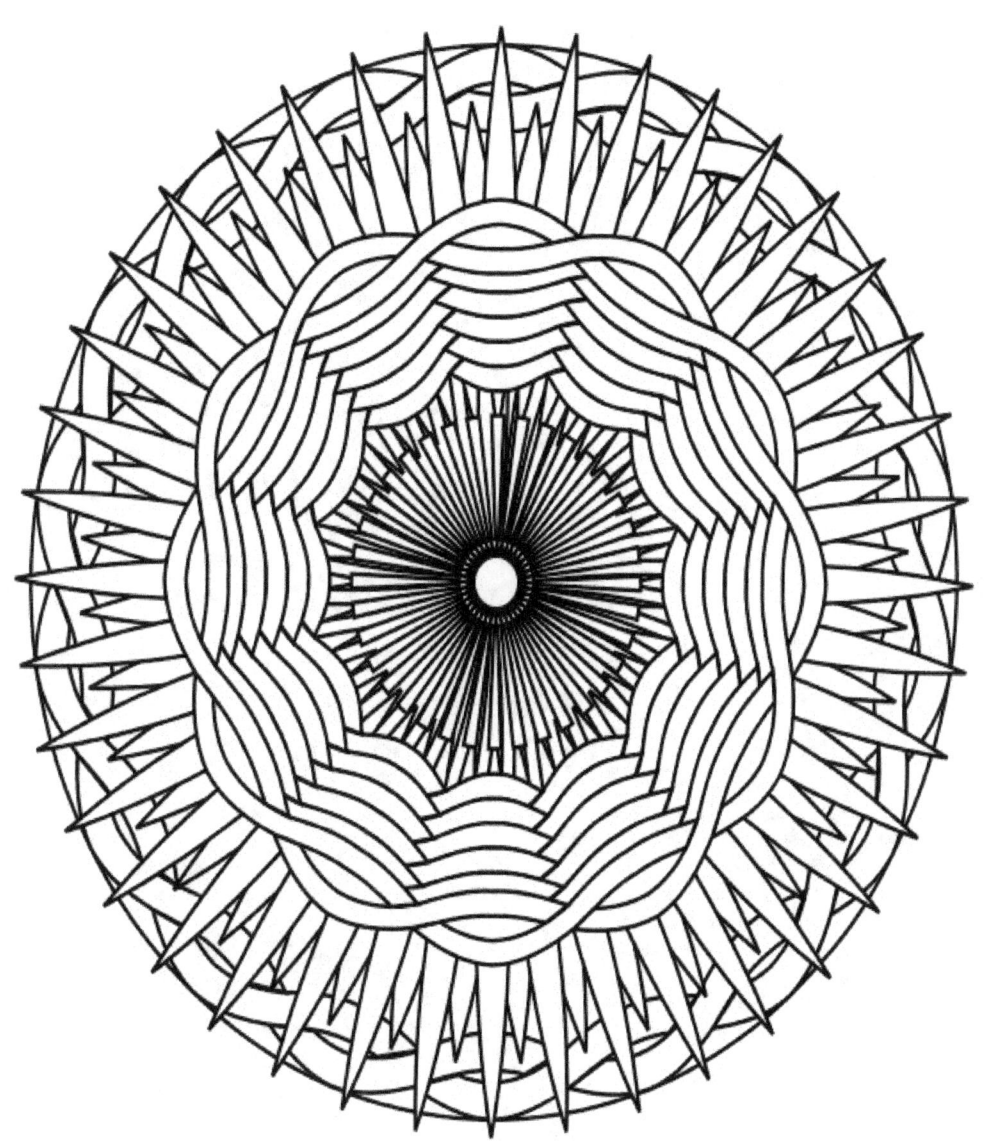

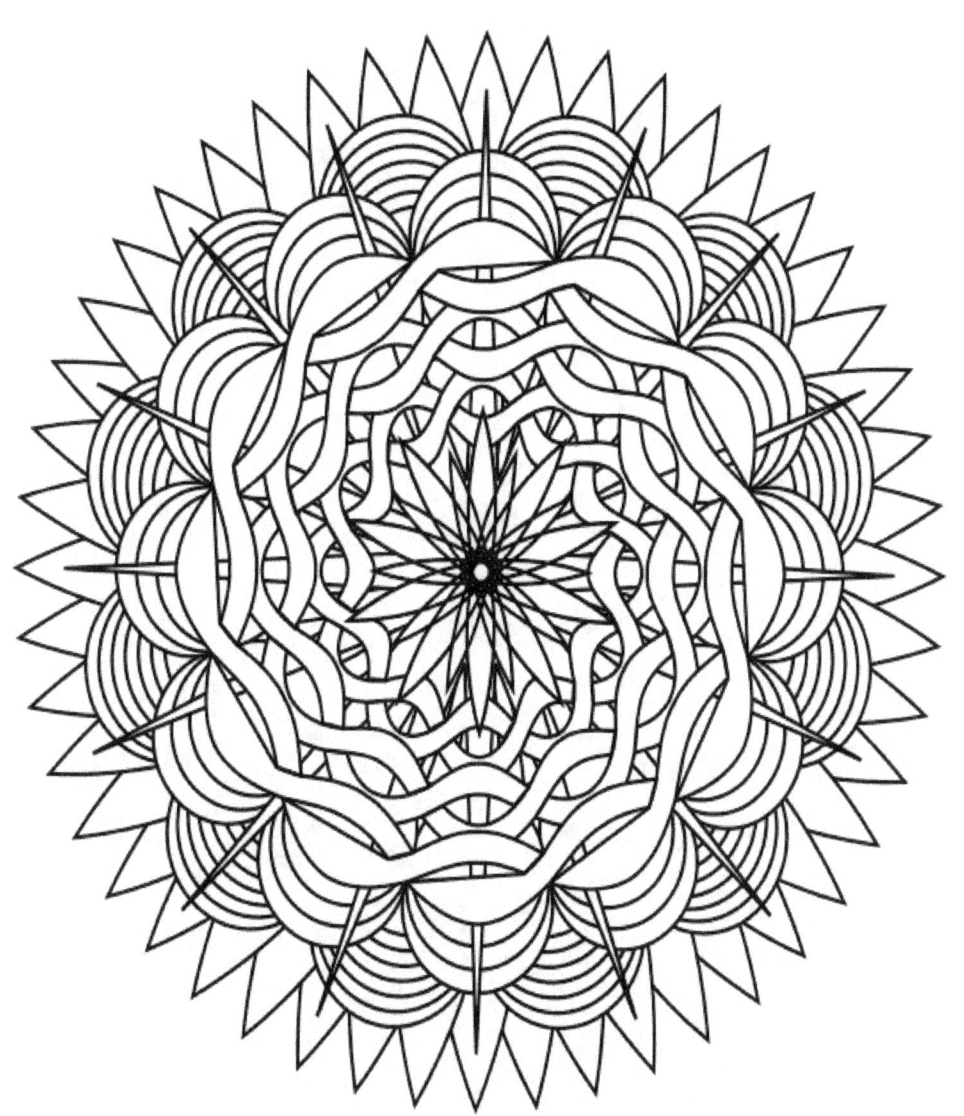

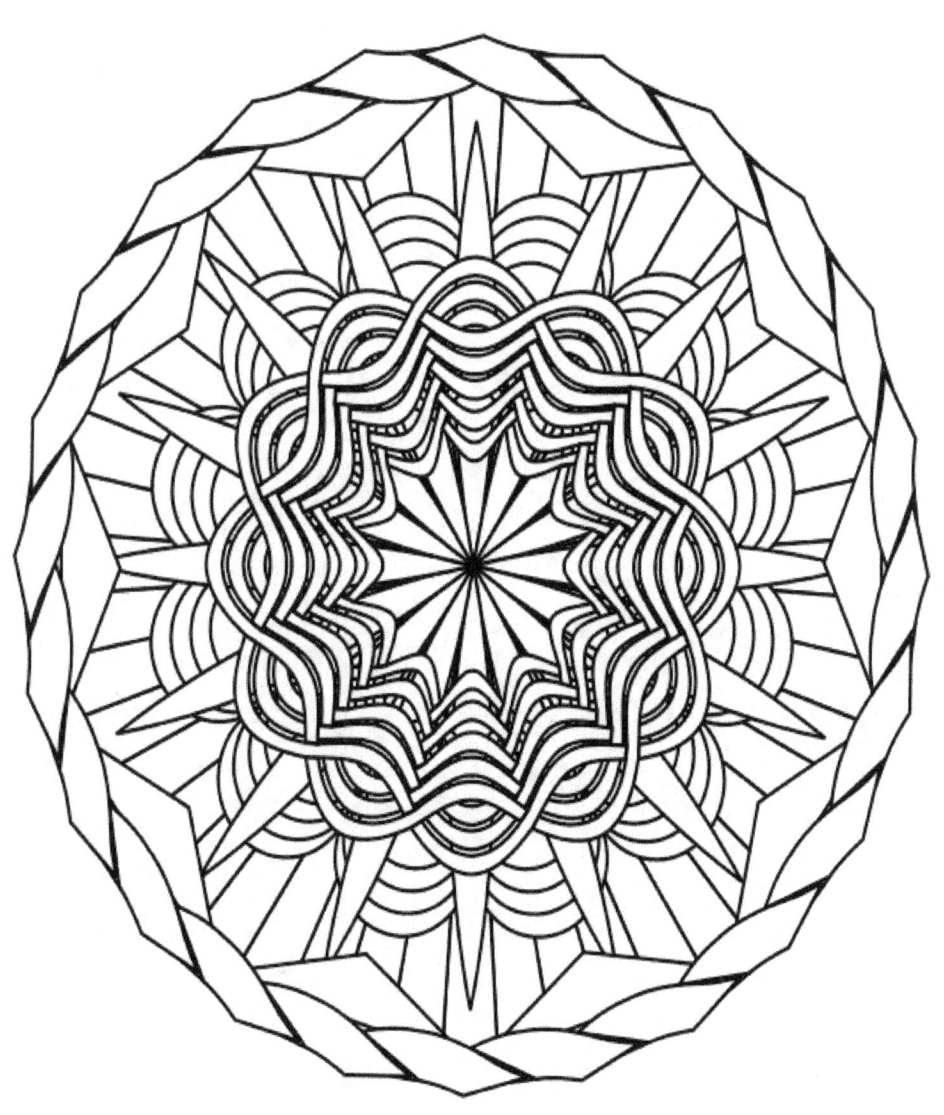

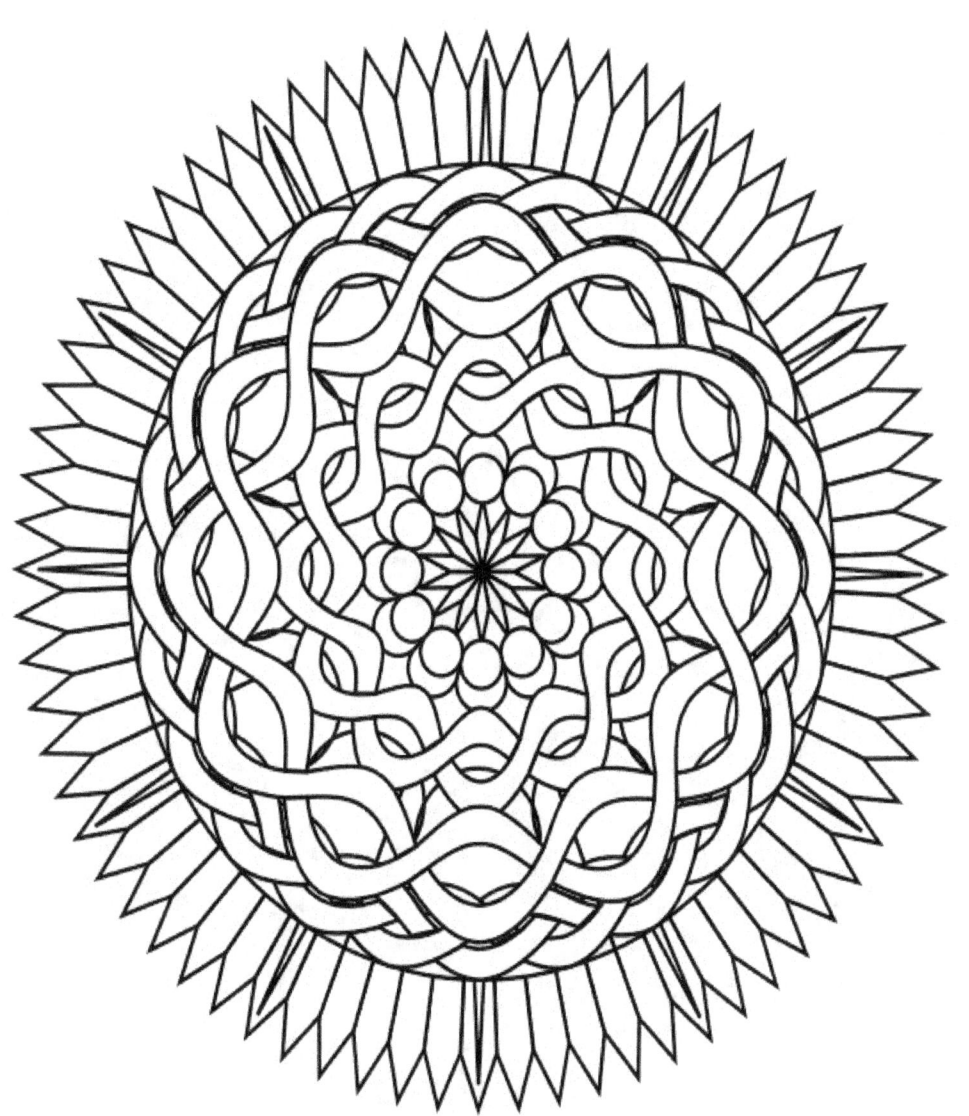

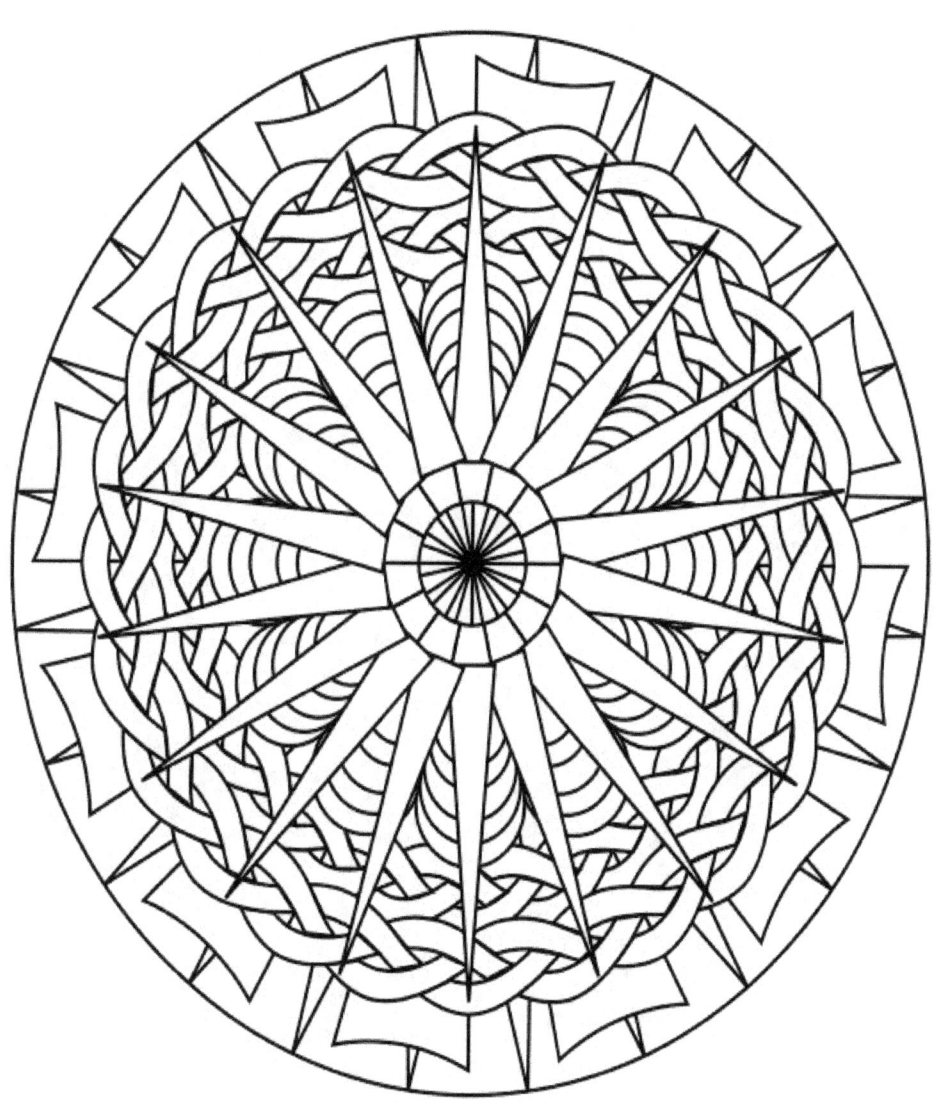

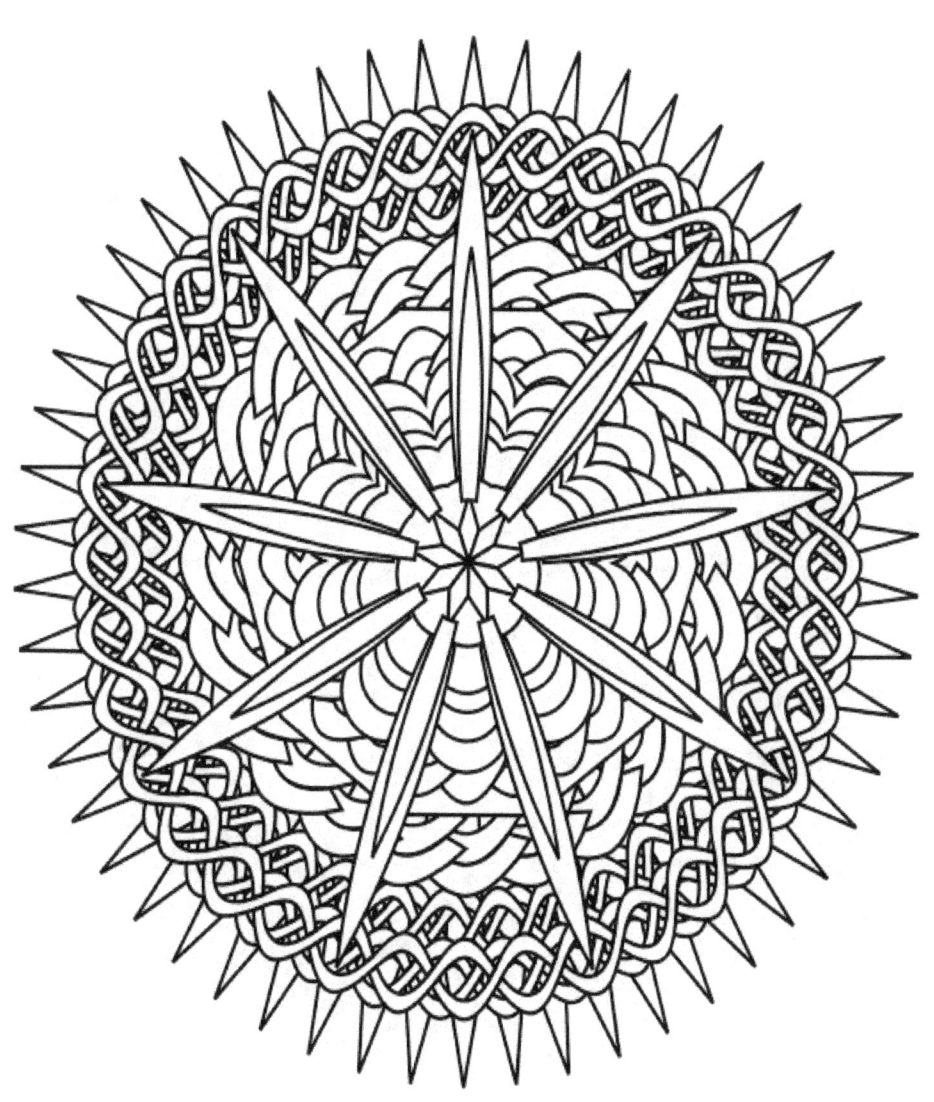

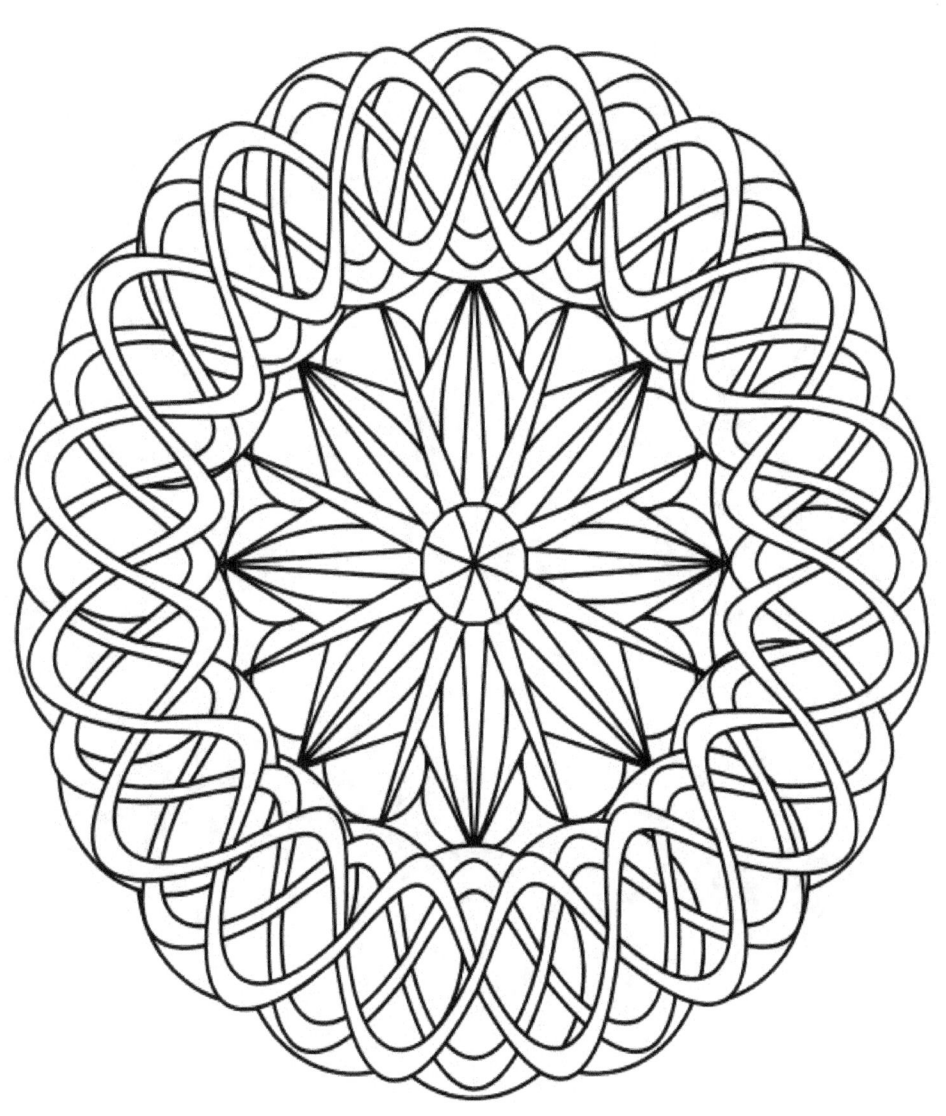

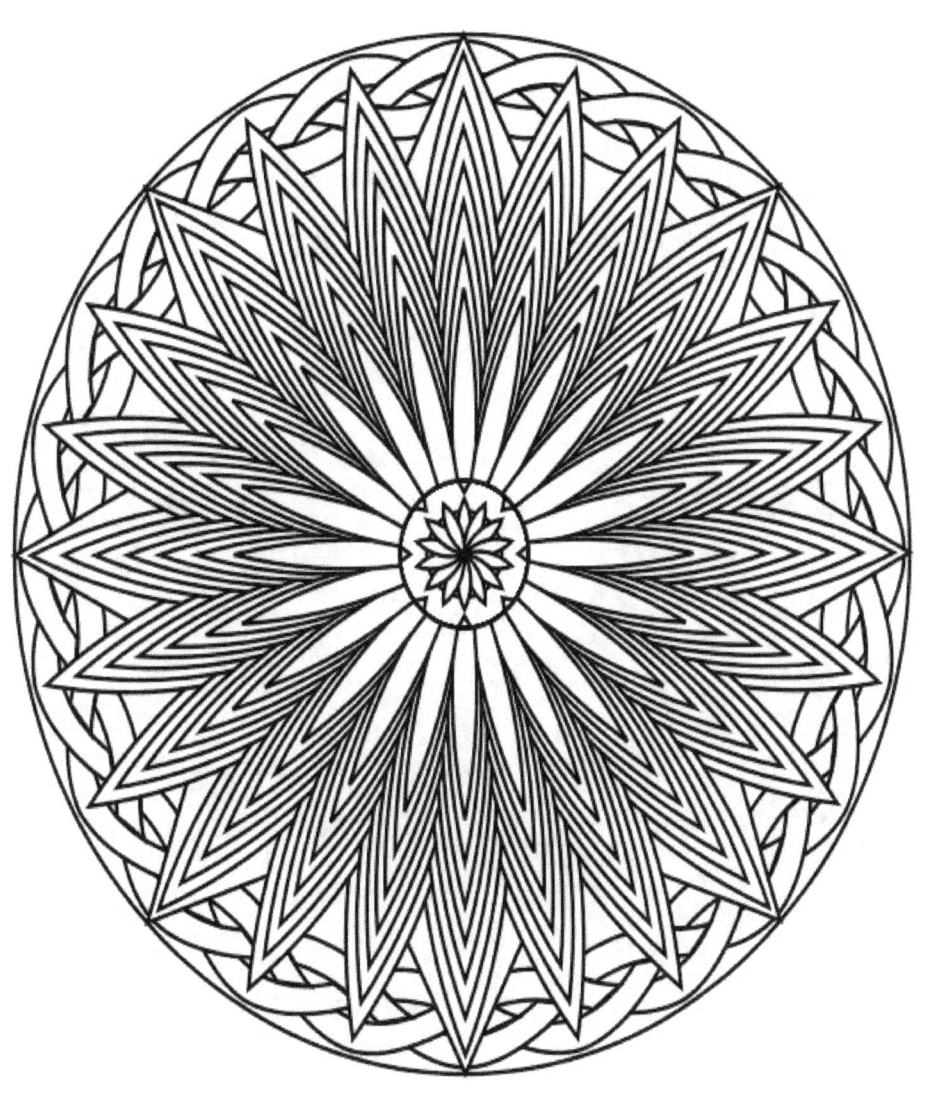

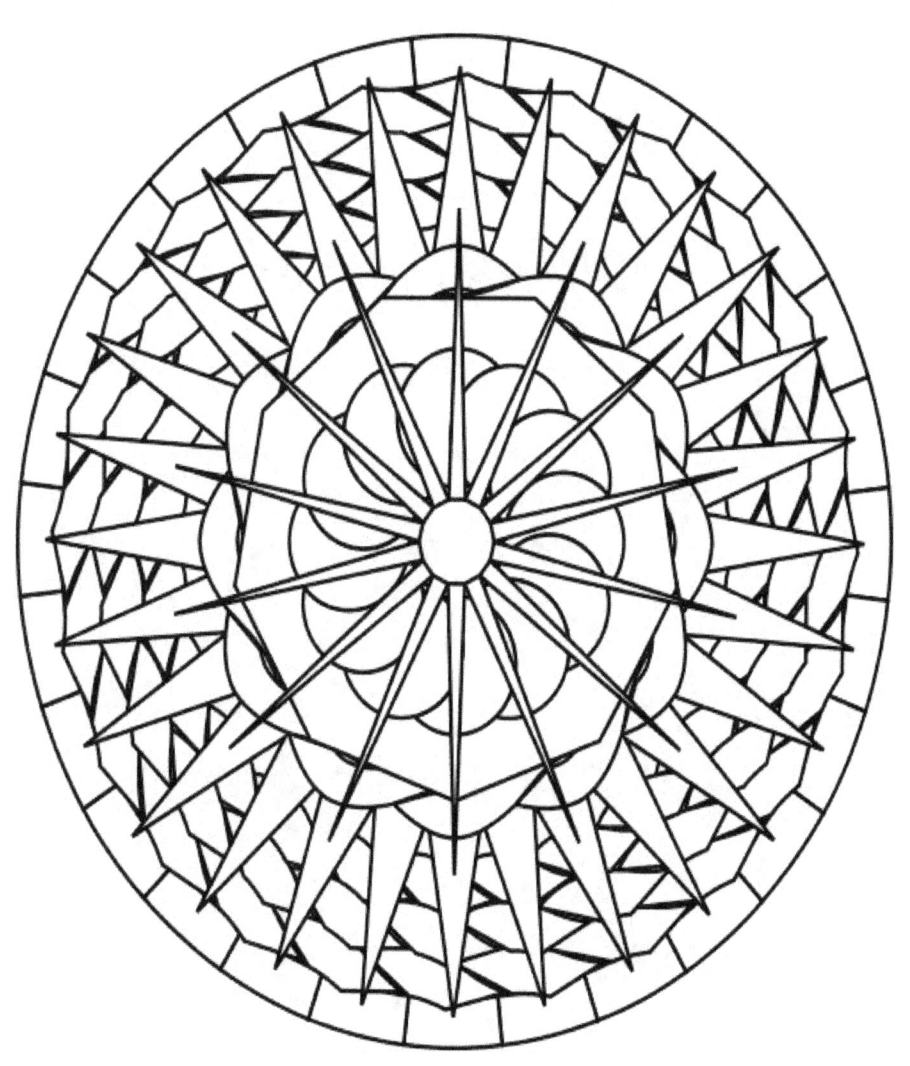

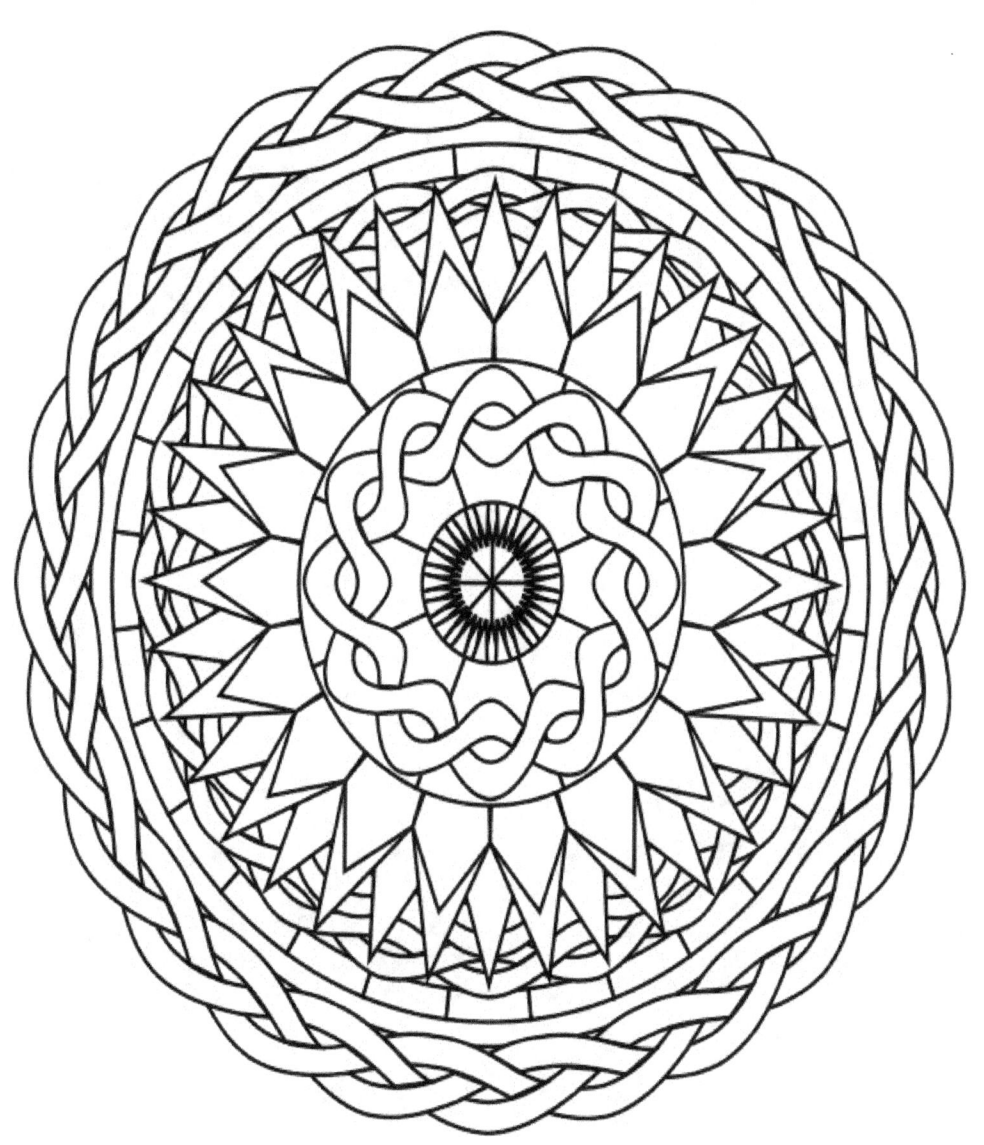

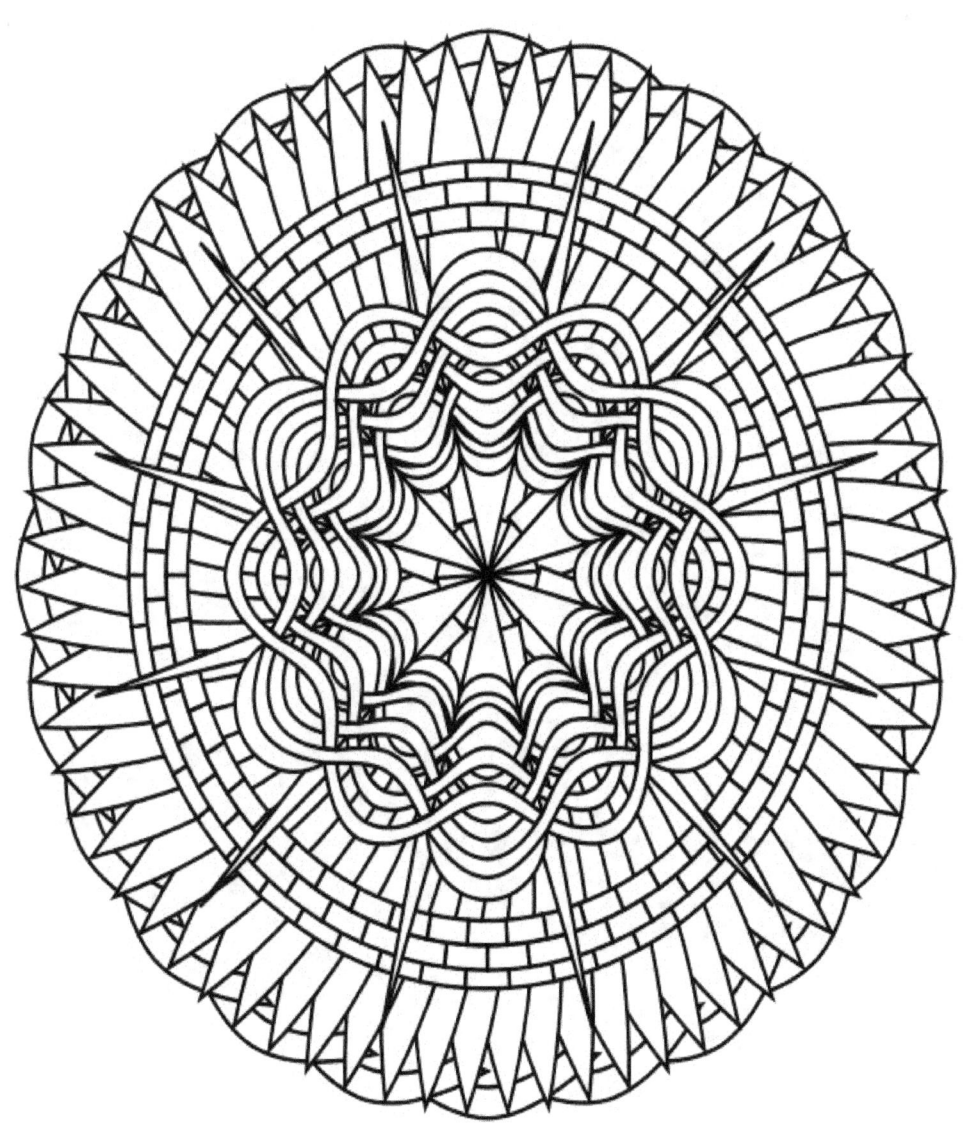

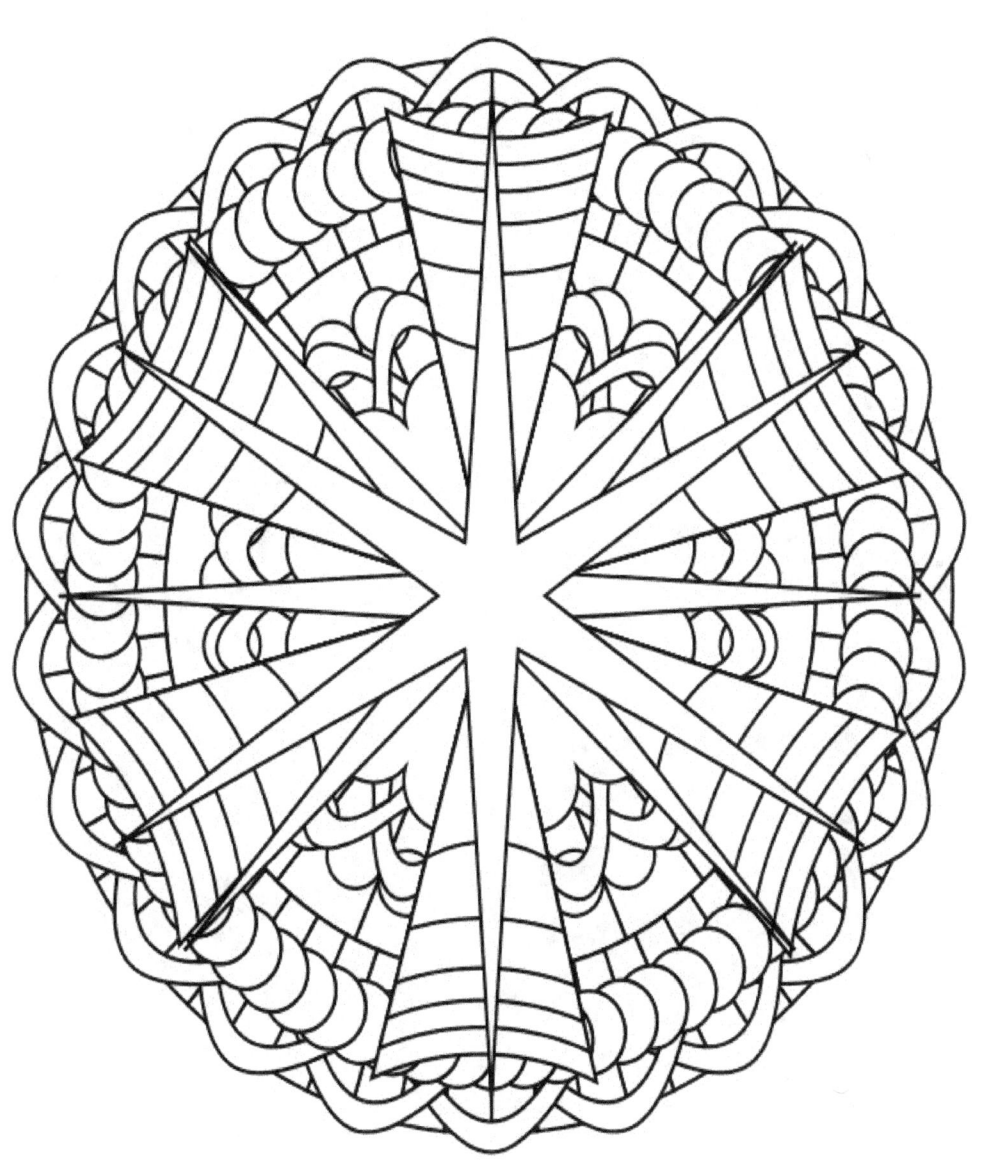

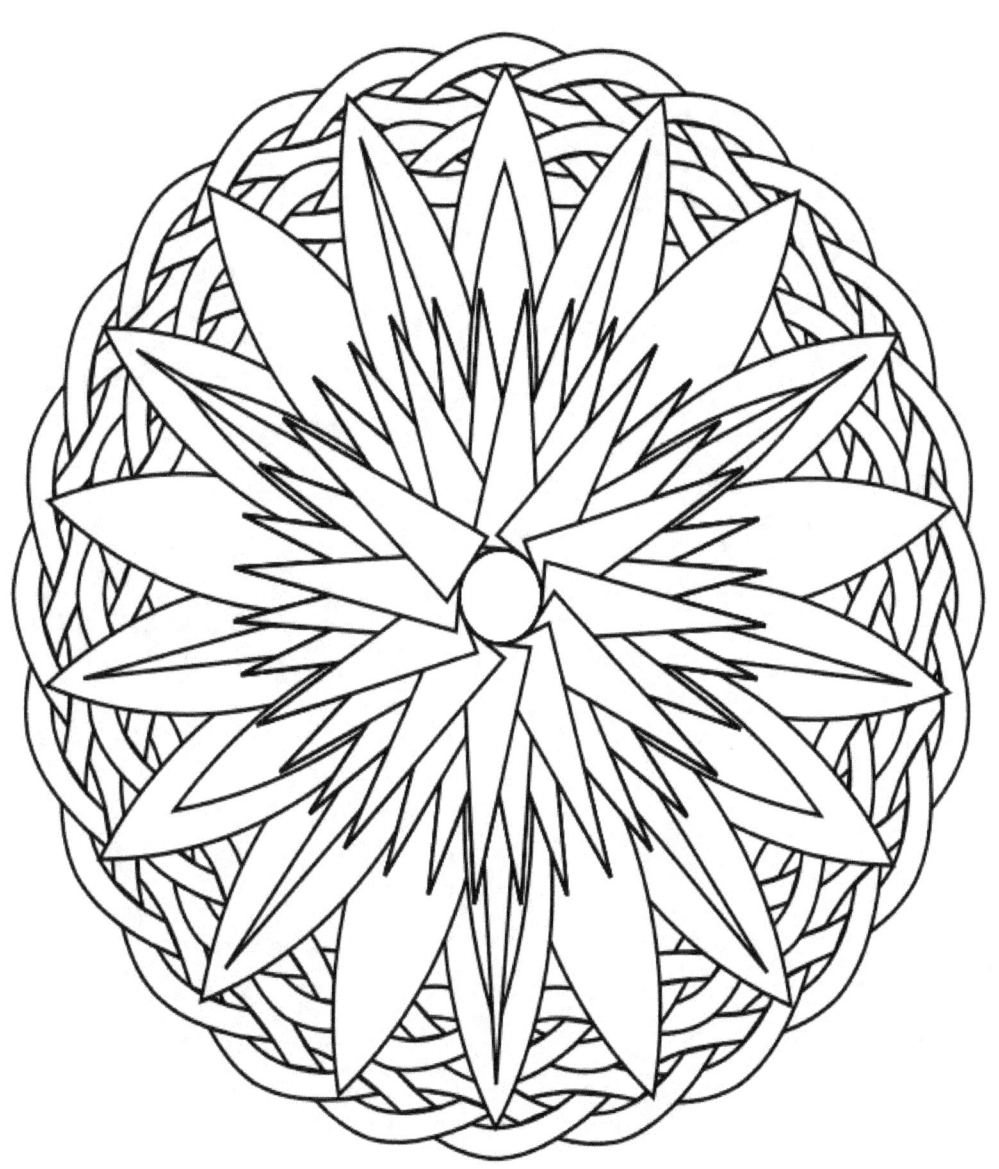

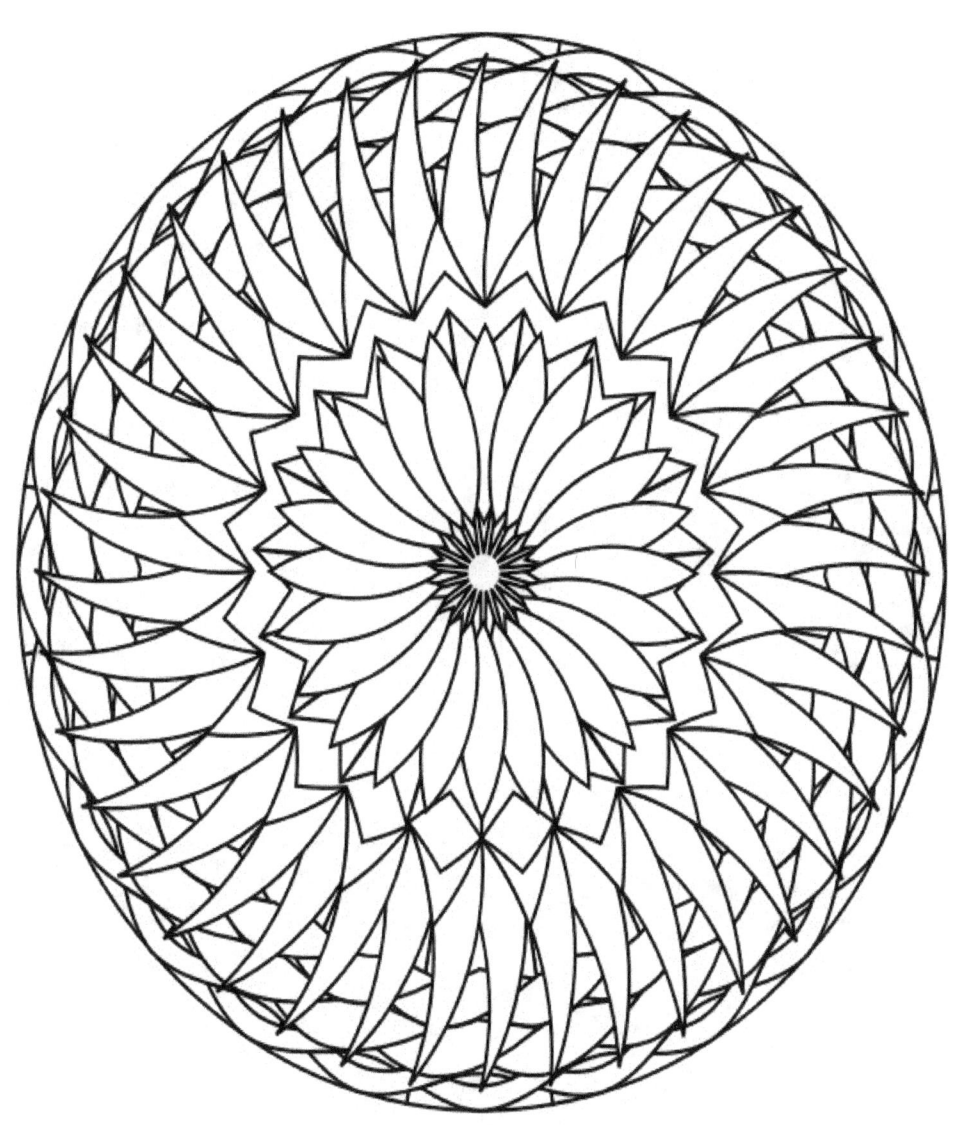

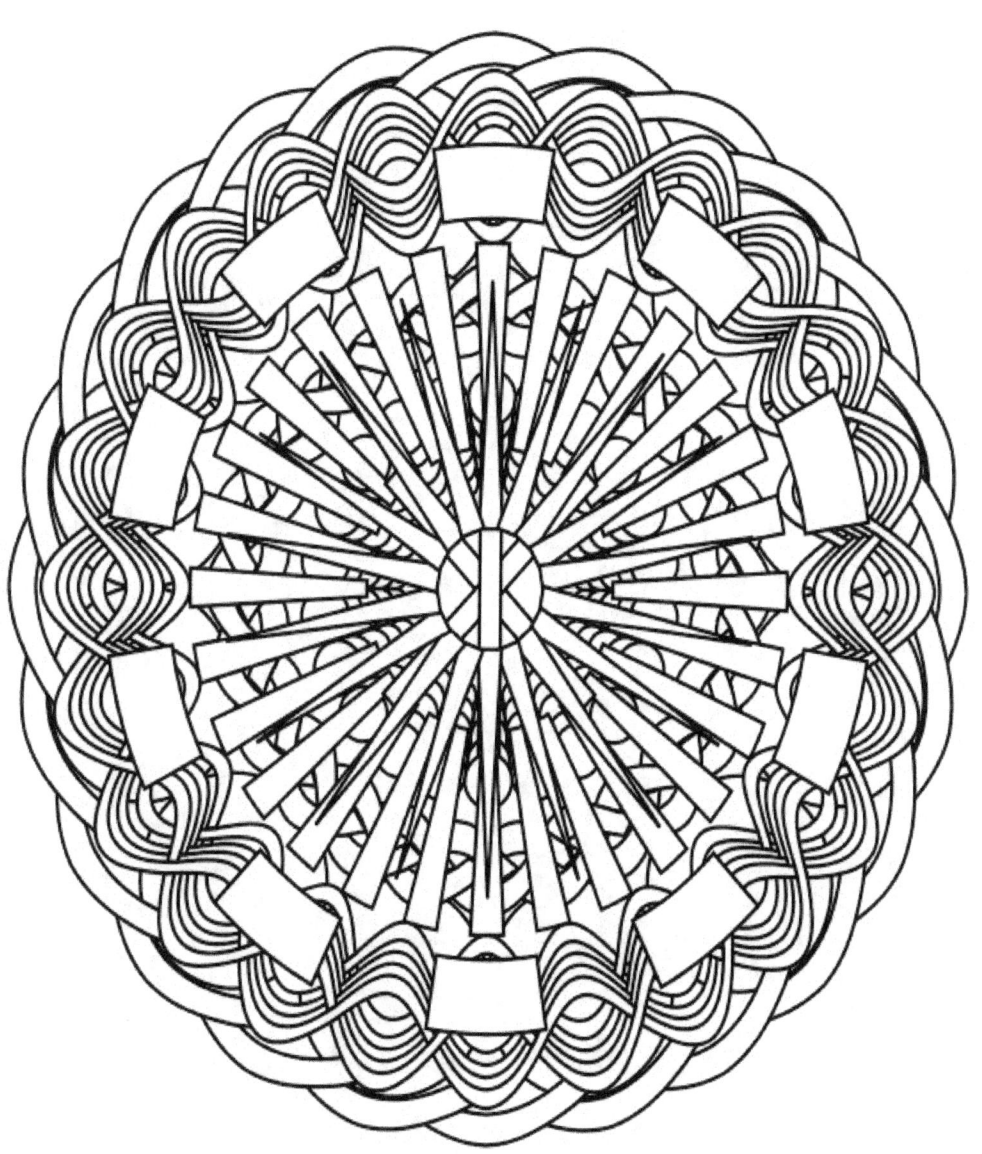

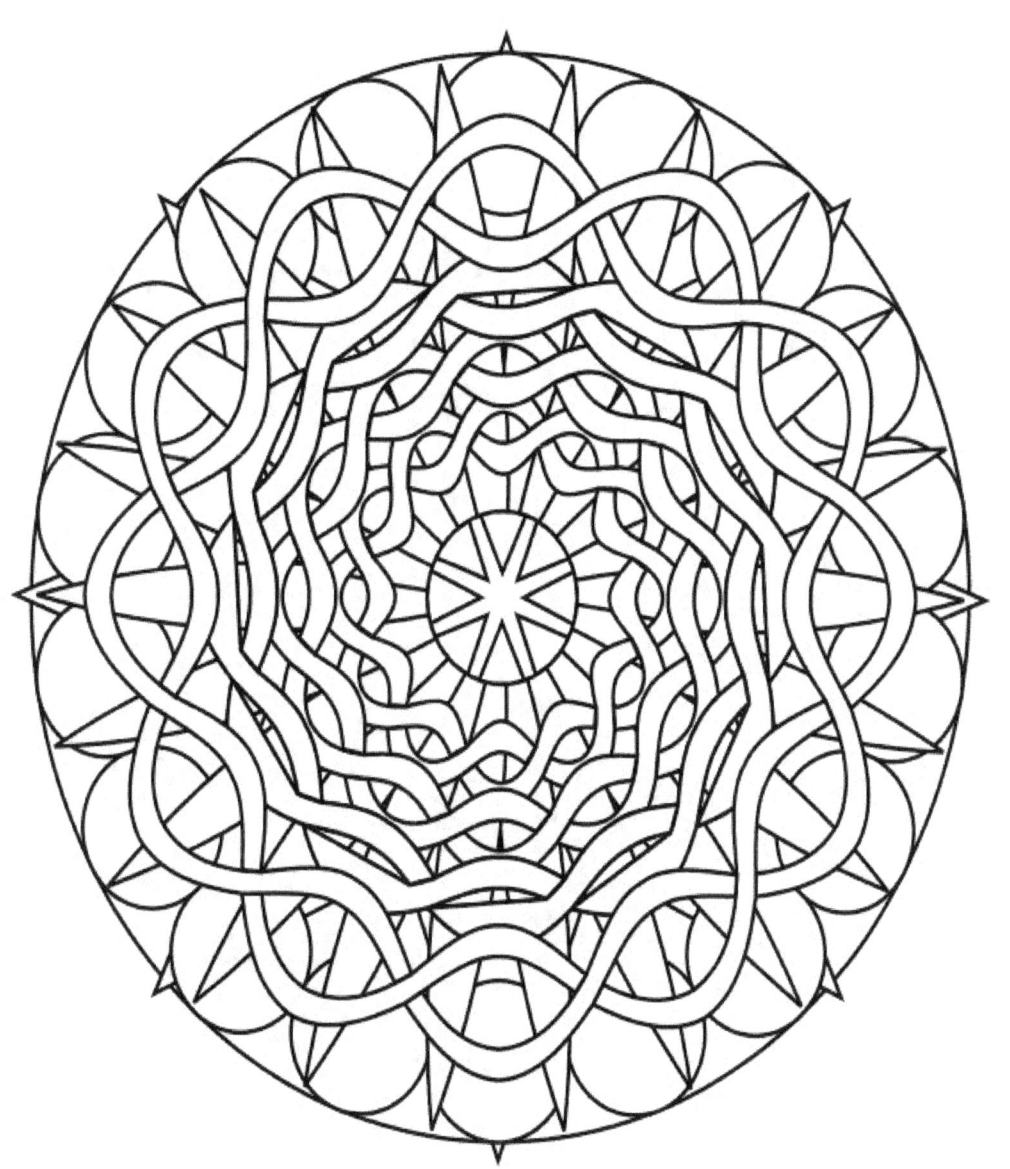

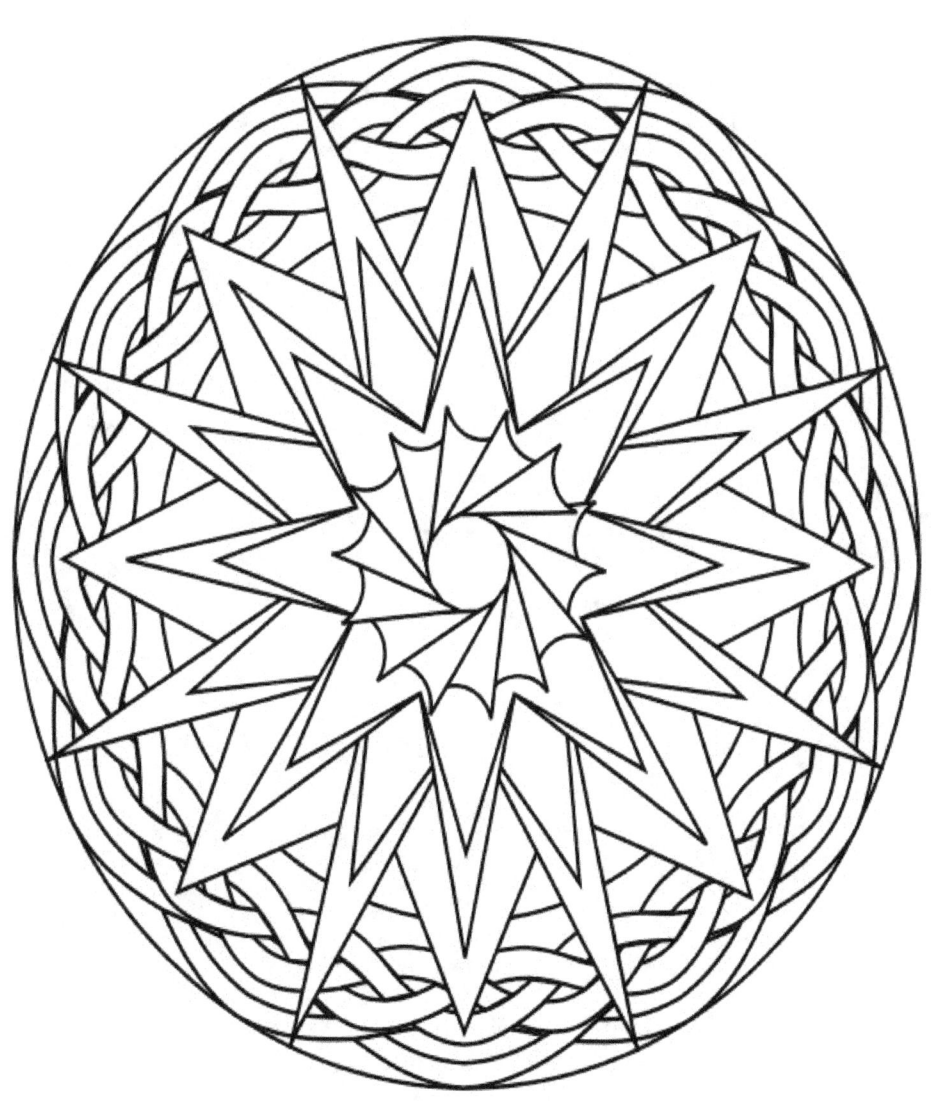

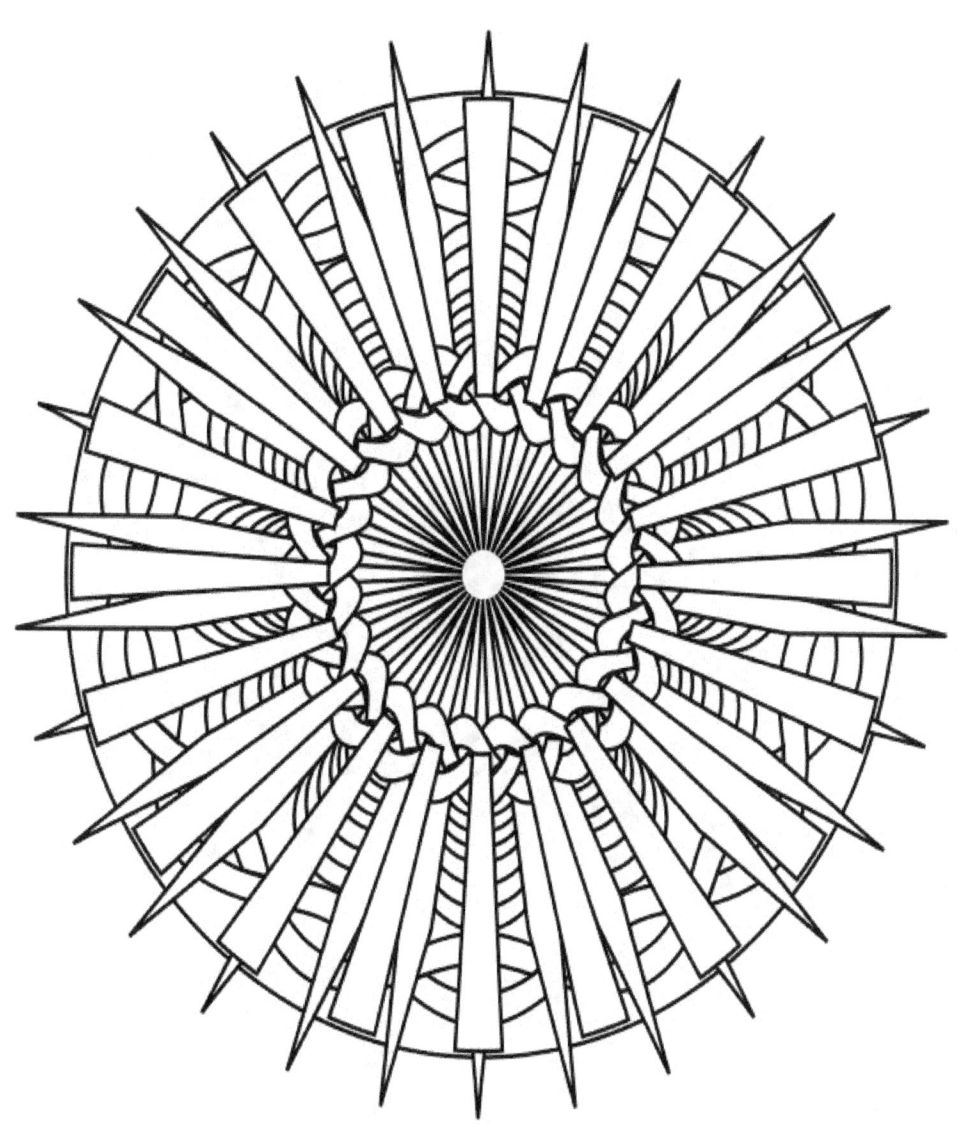

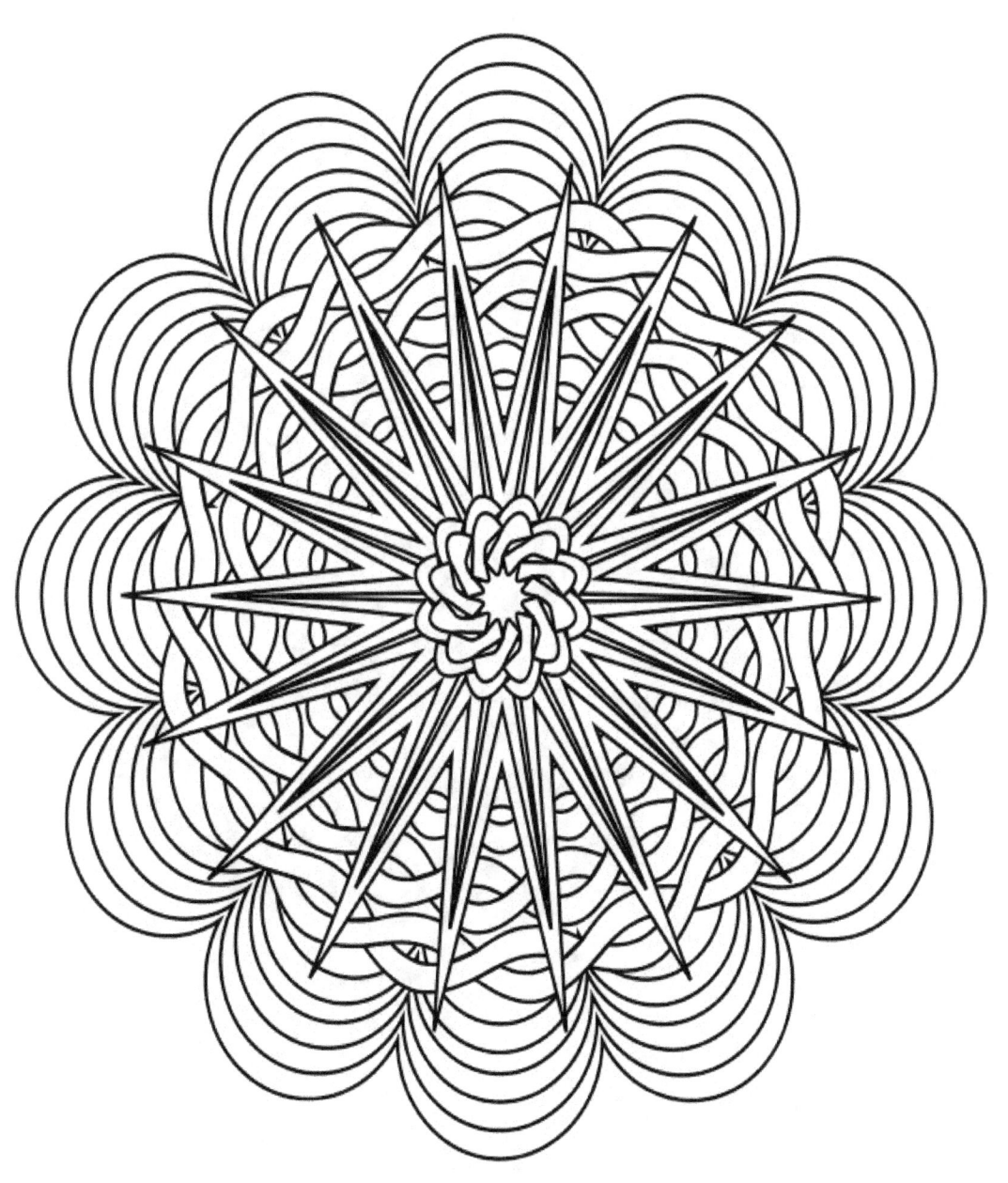

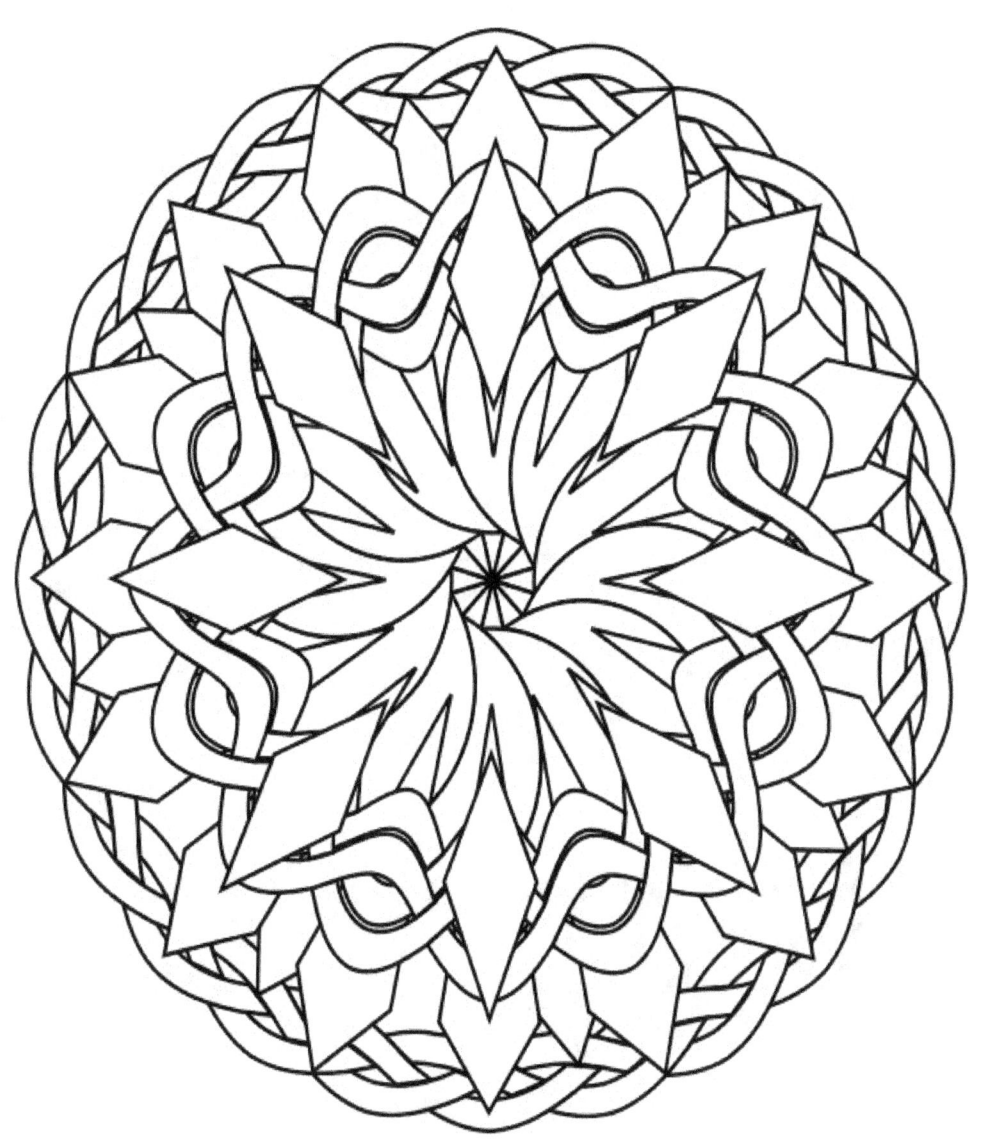

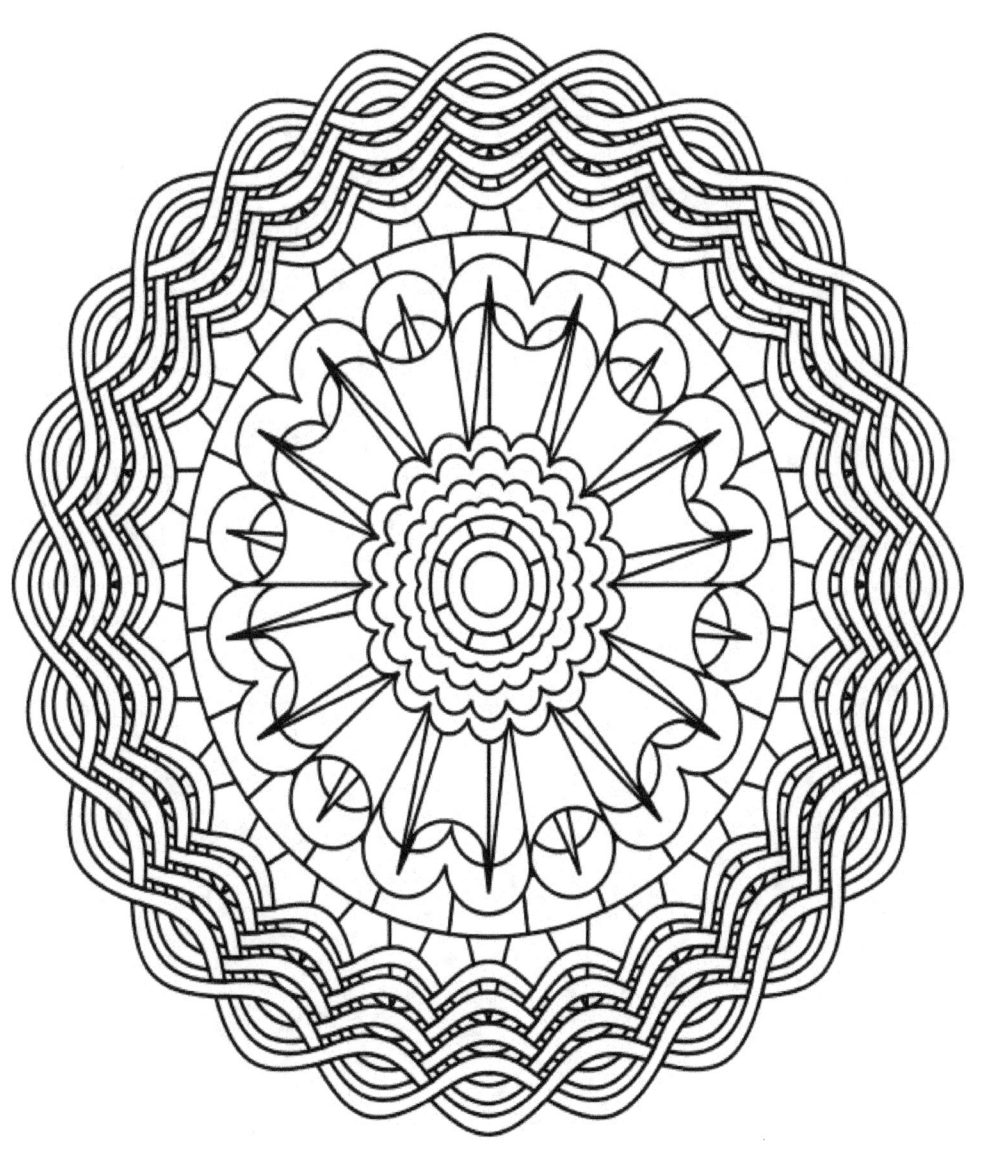

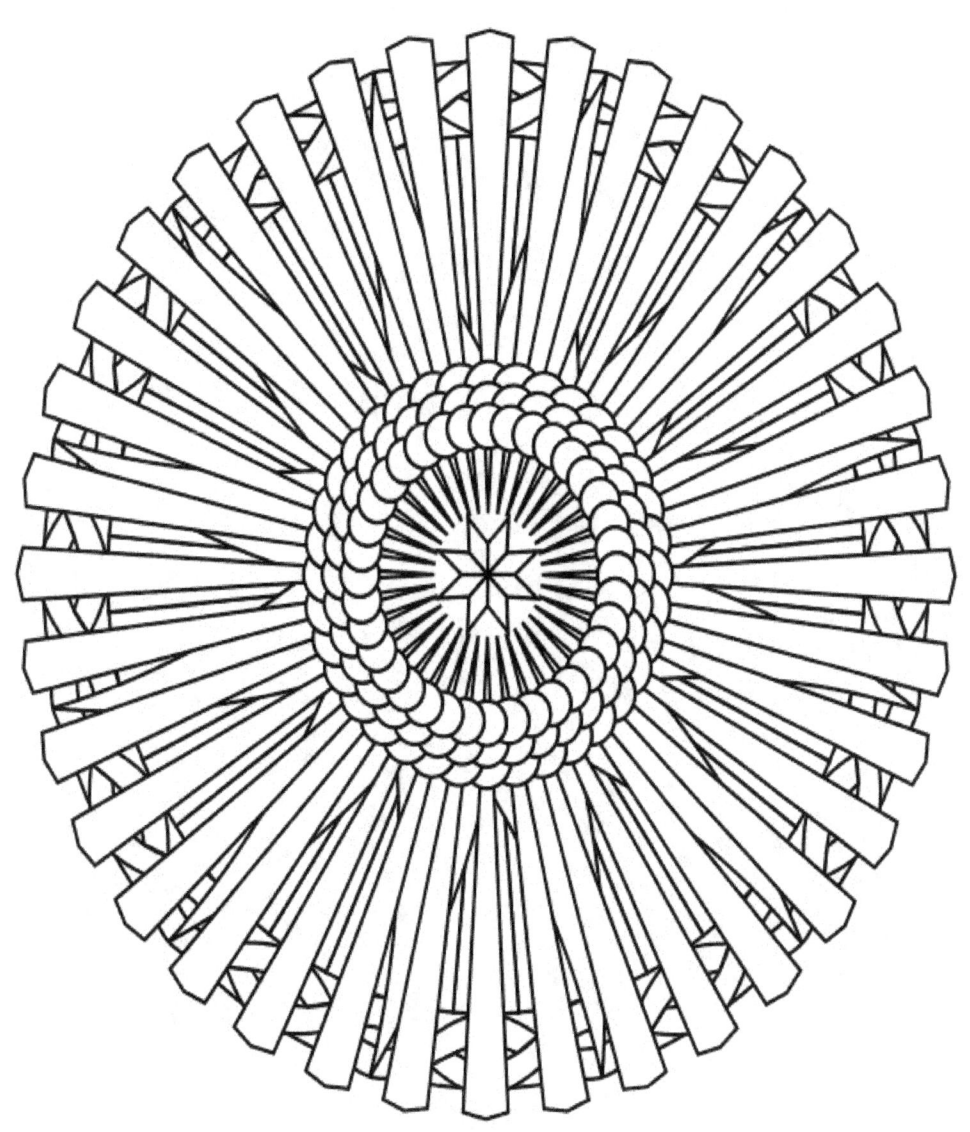

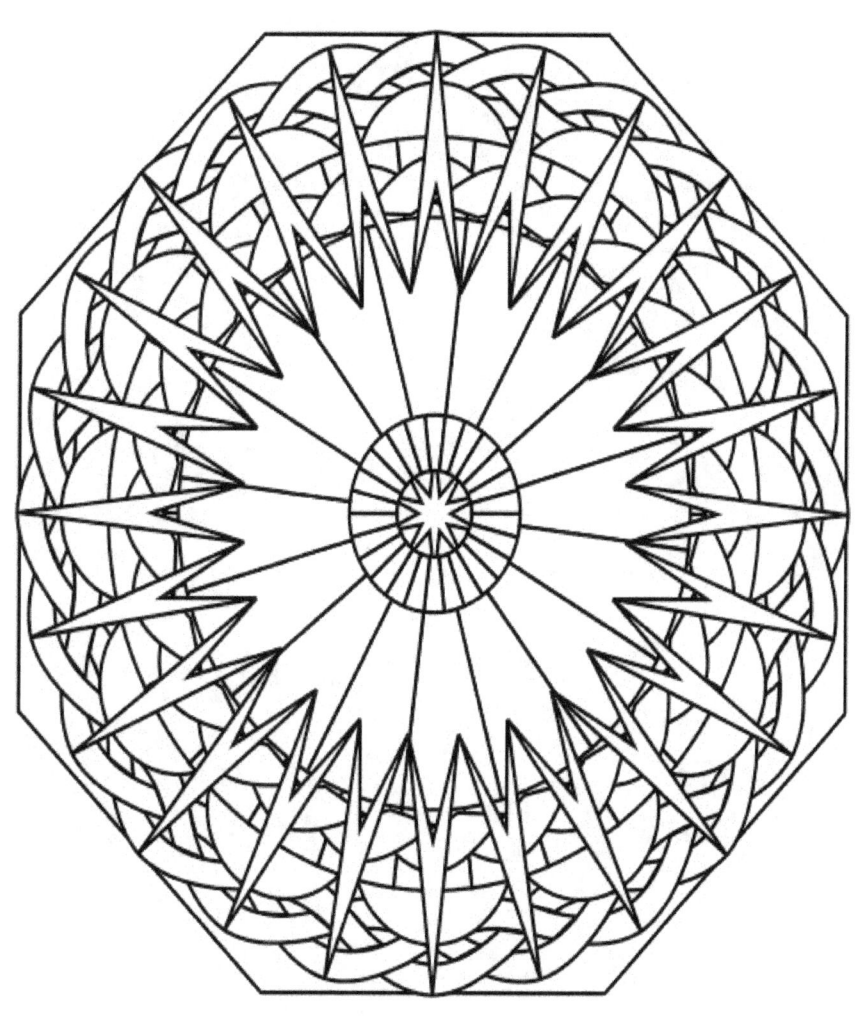

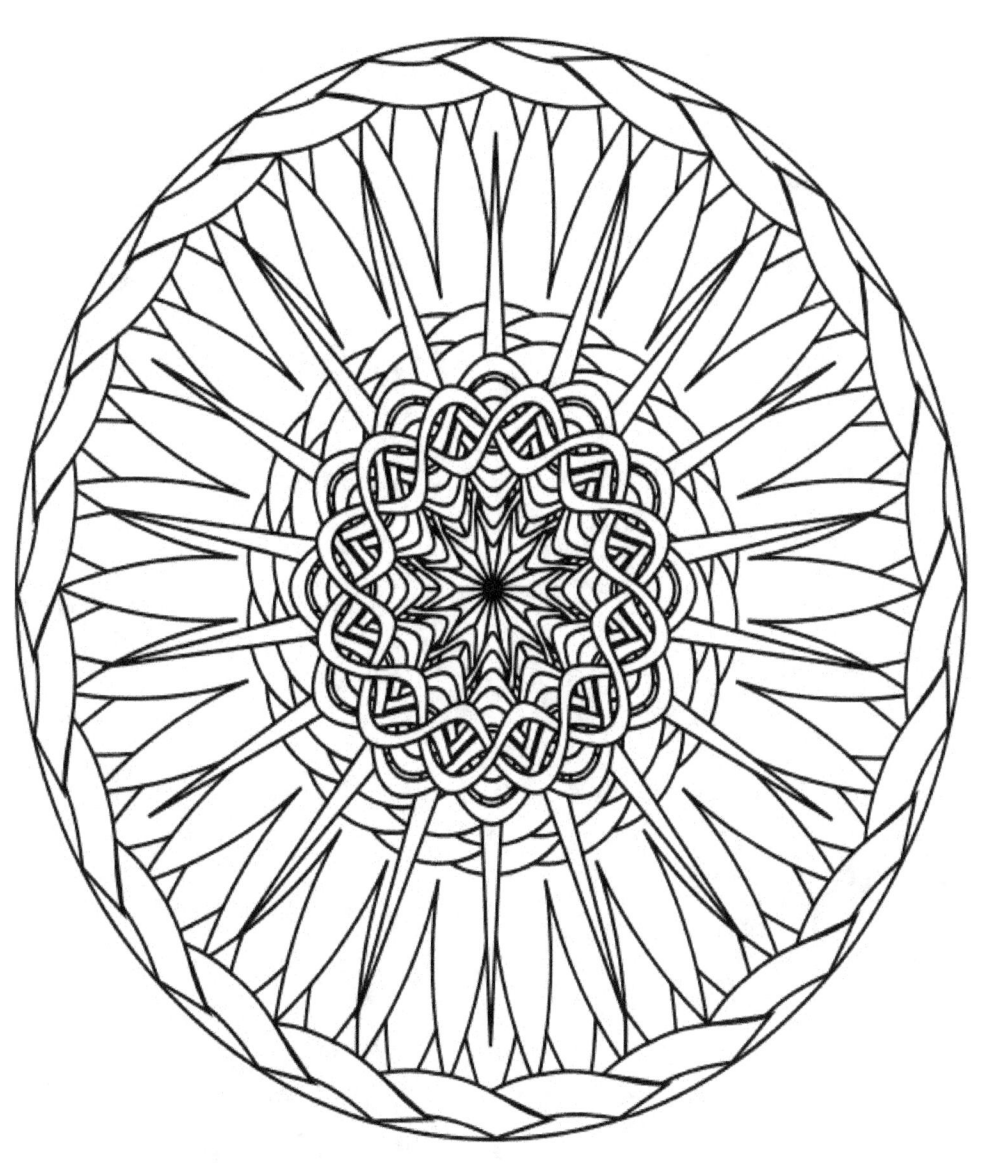

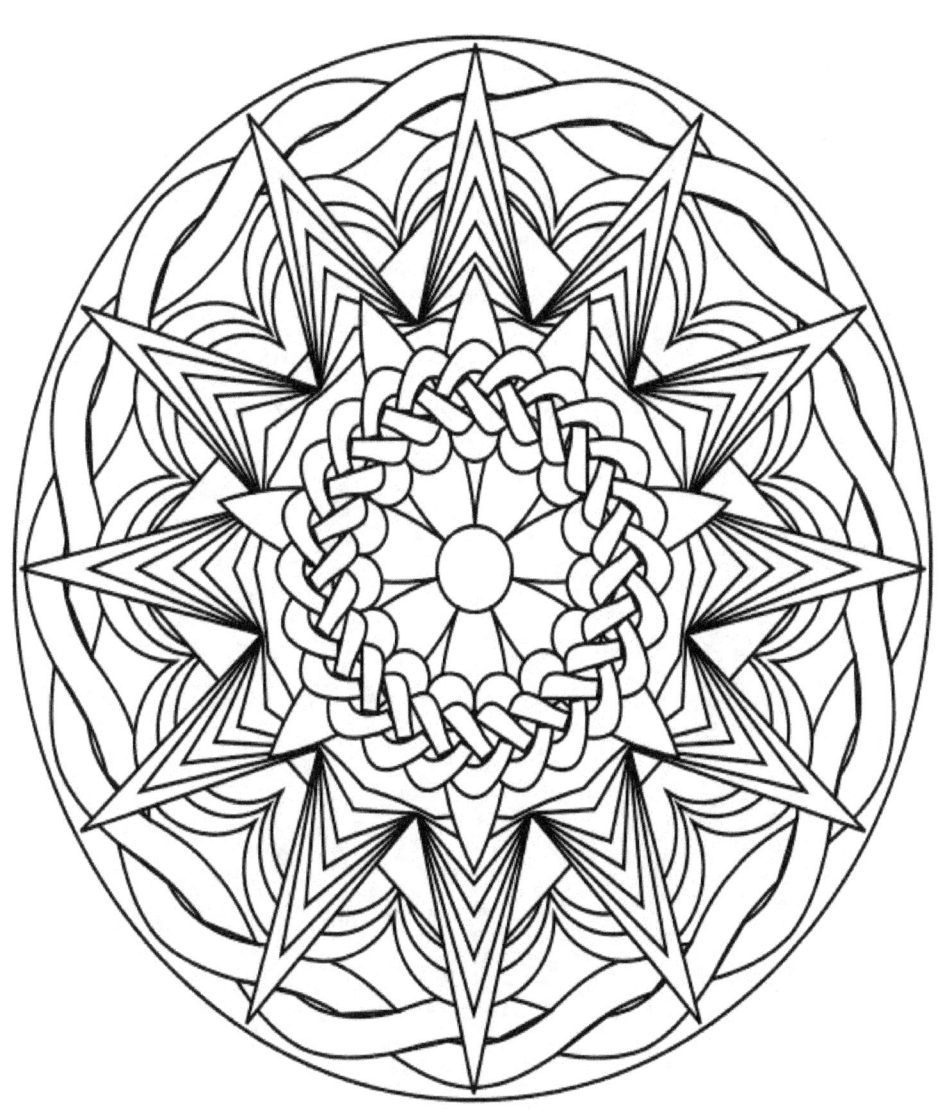

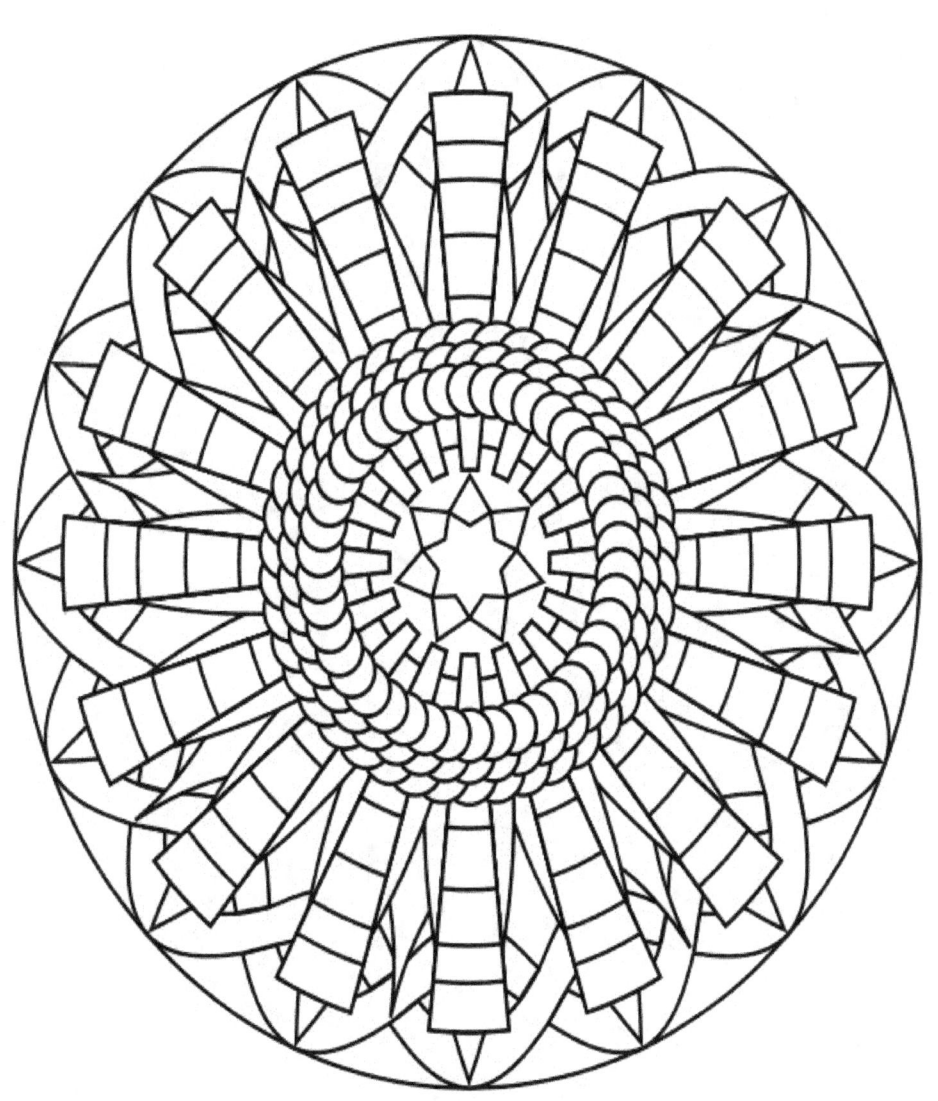

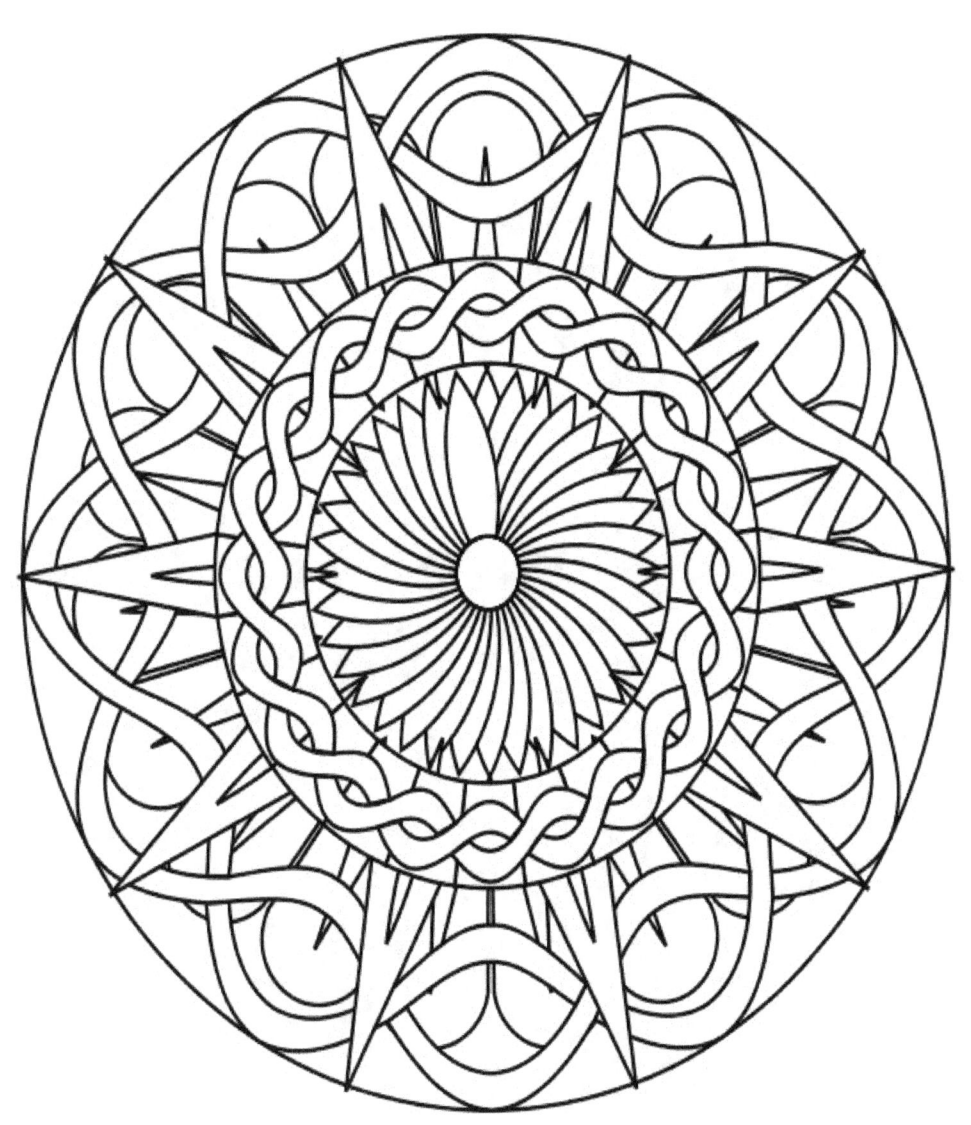

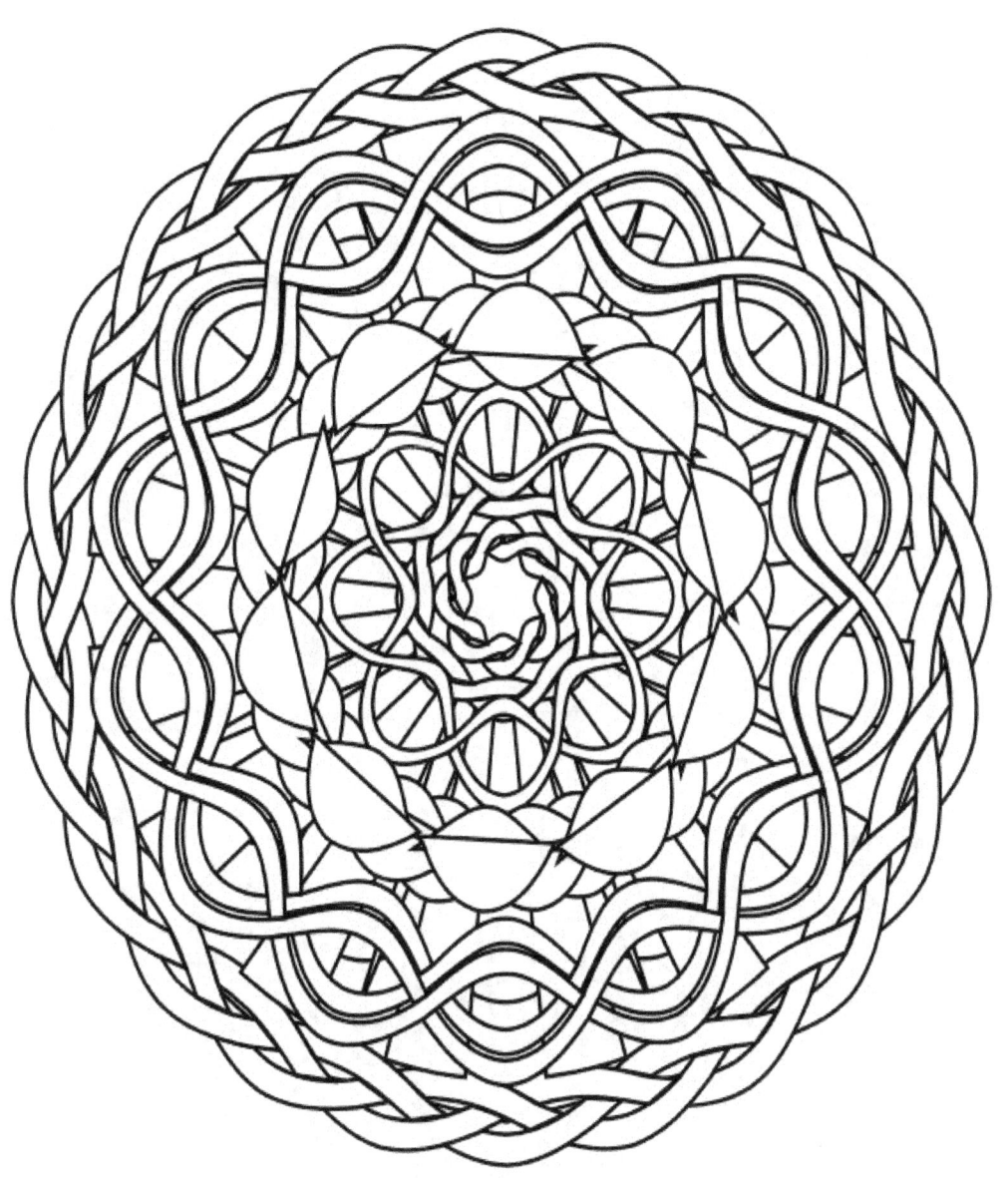

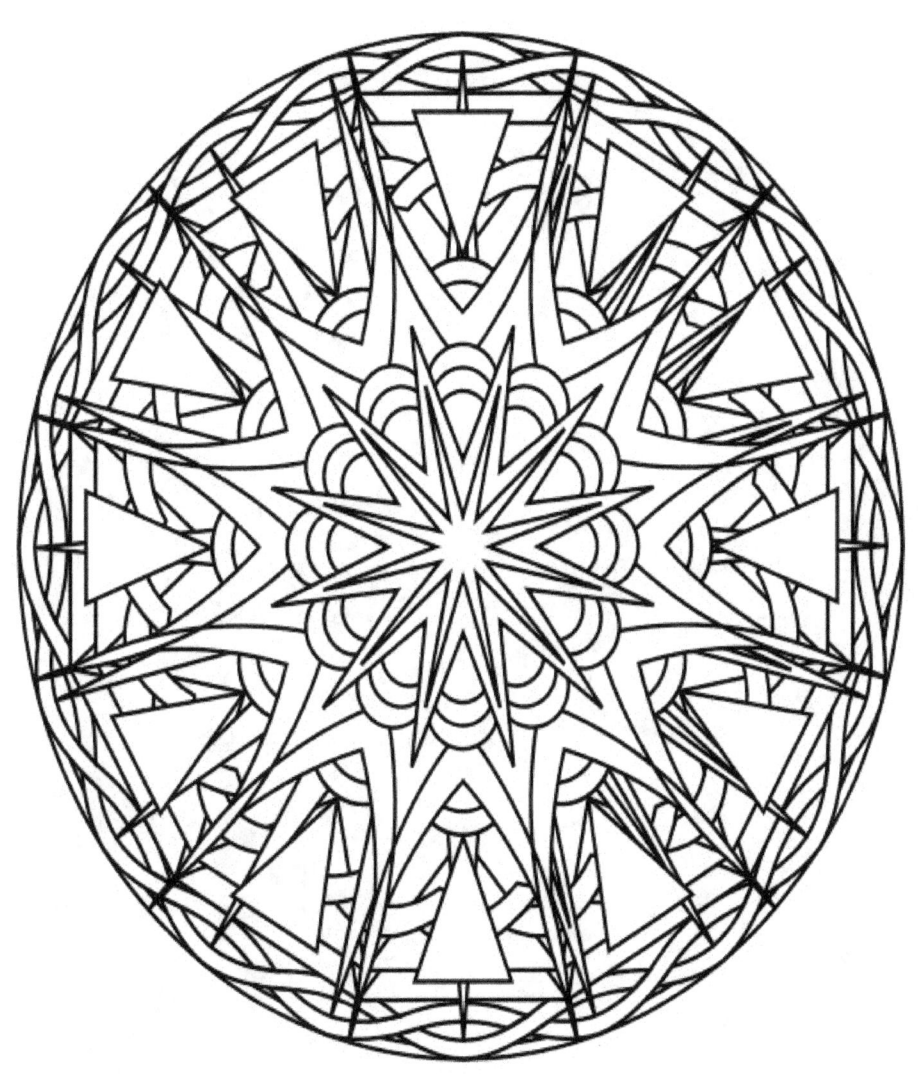

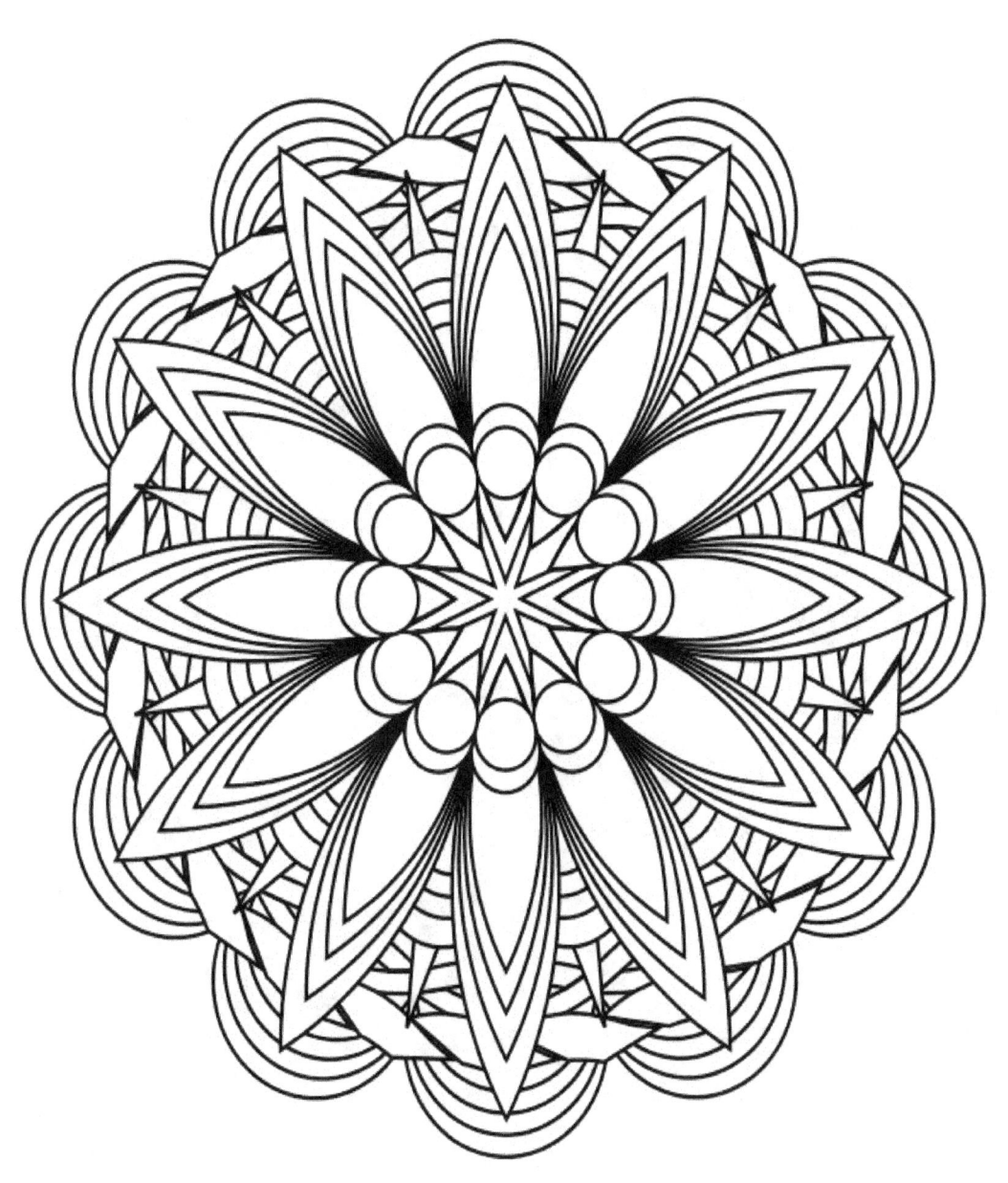

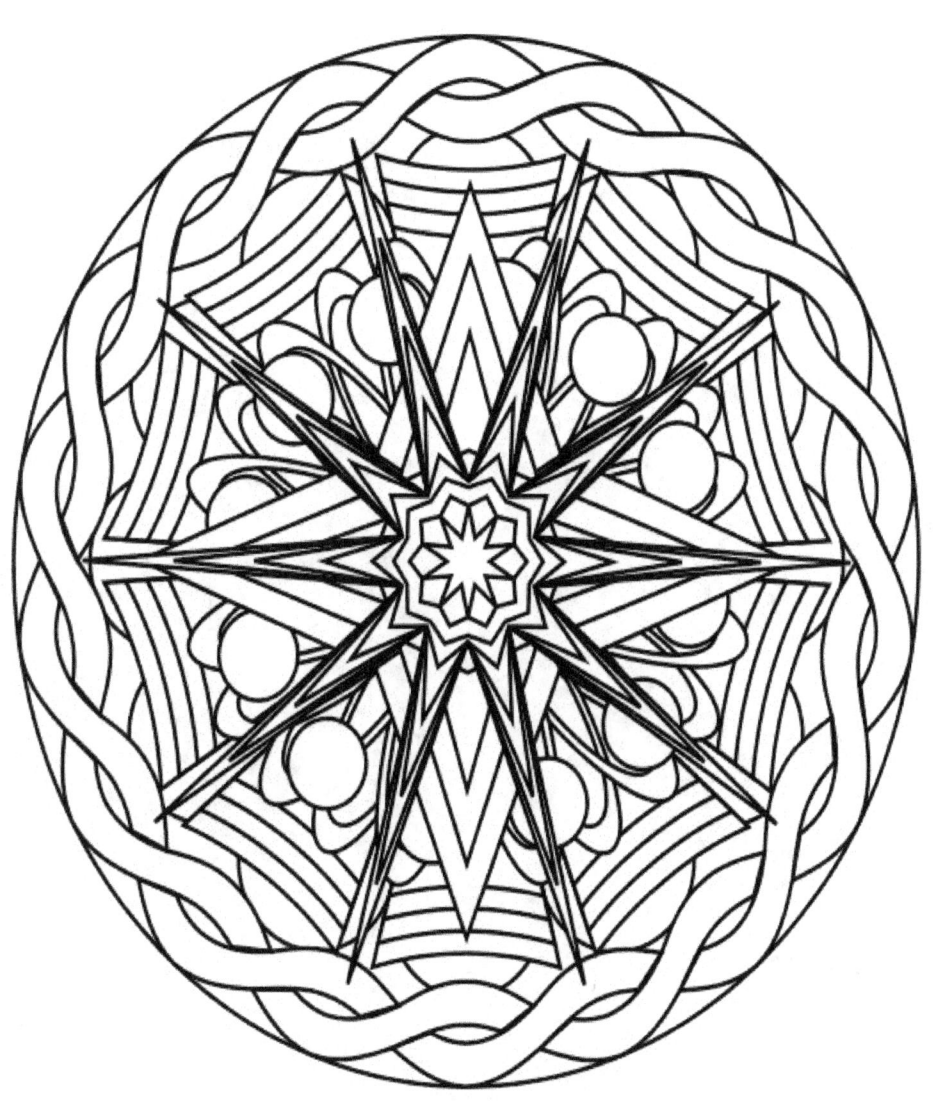

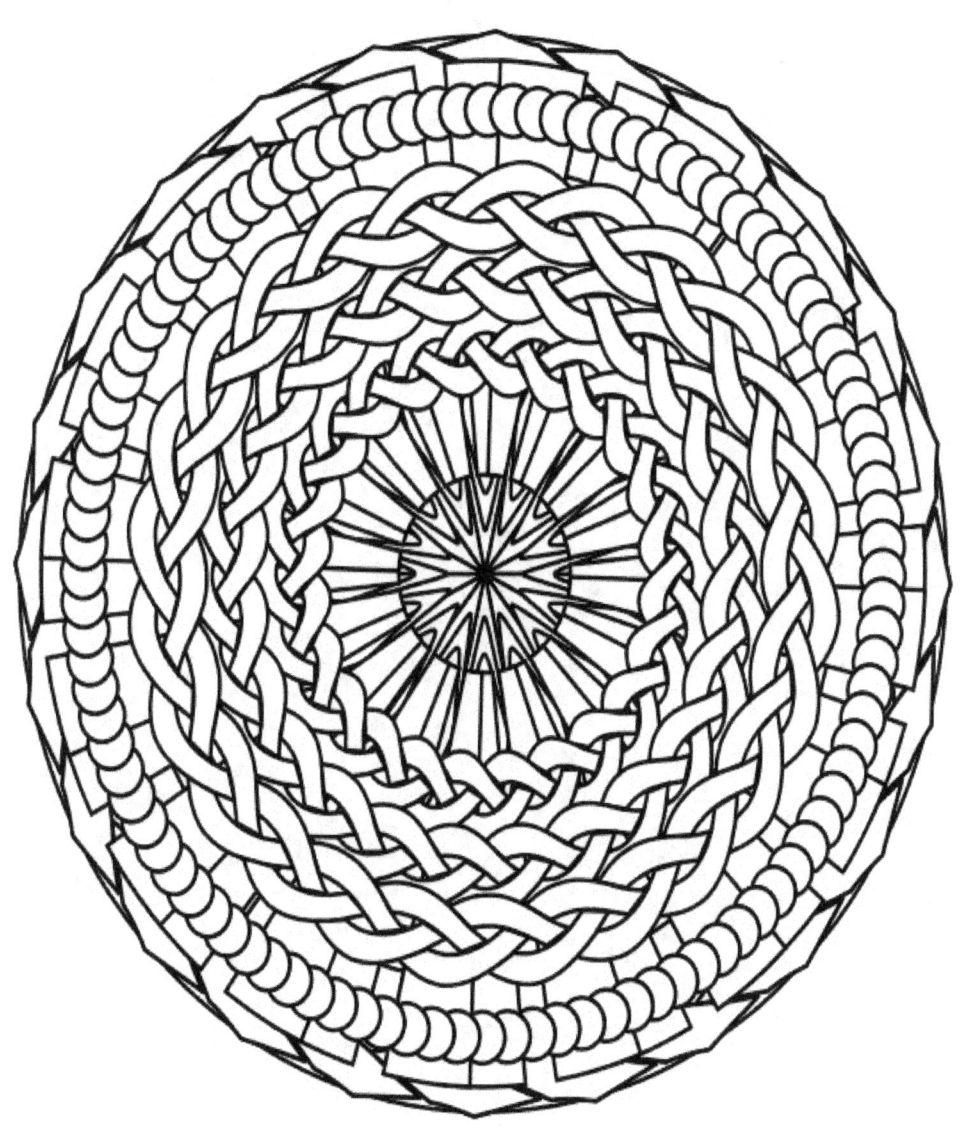

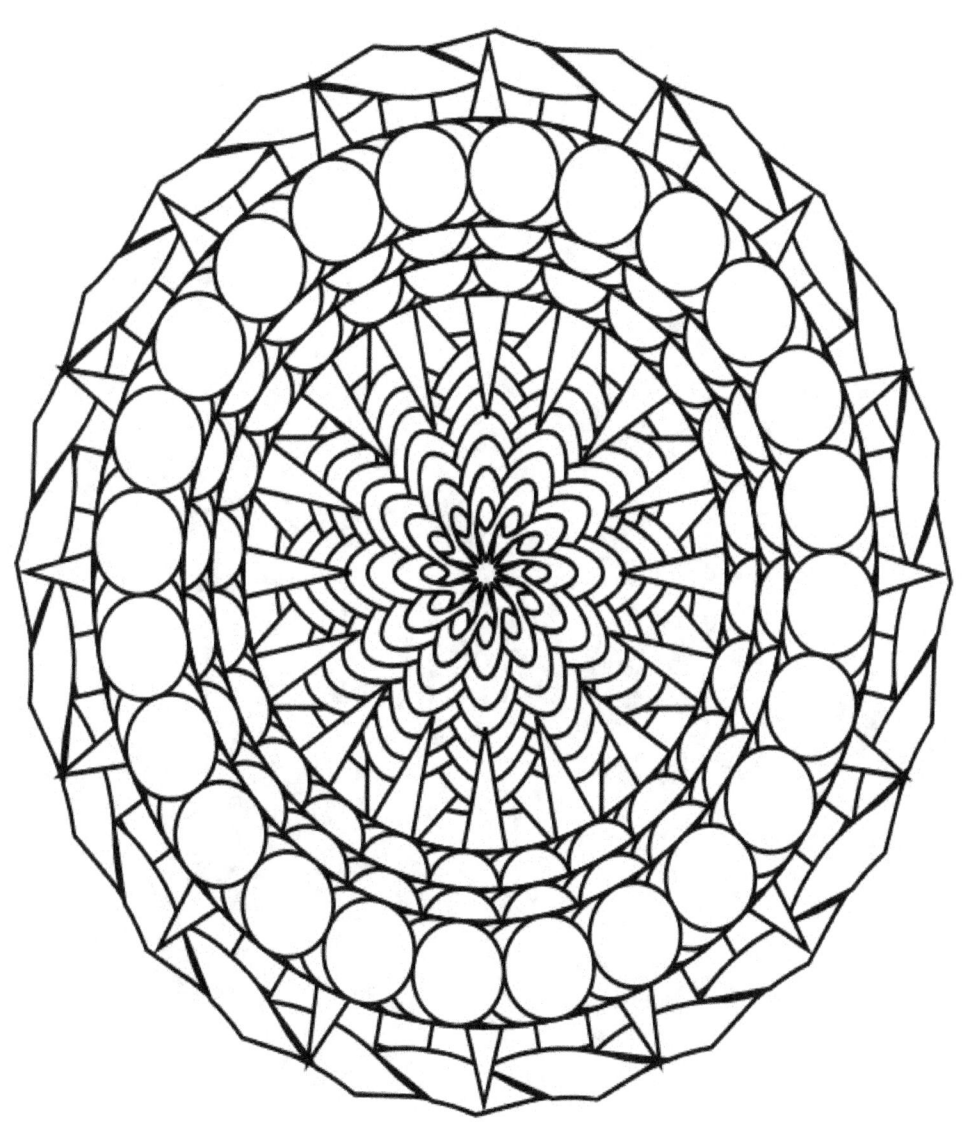

Thanks again for your time.

I hope you will be back for my next book.

For bonus pages and to get information on new books, visit

Amazon.com/Jeffrey-Littorno/e/B004UMNNVW

Or www.facebook.com/jlittorno.

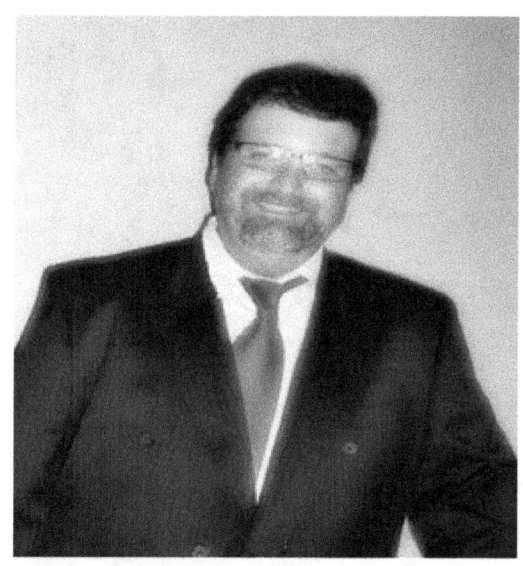

Jeffrey Littorno

www.ingramcontent.com/pod-product-compliance
Lightning Source LLC
Chambersburg PA
CBHW081507170526

45166CB00008B/2576